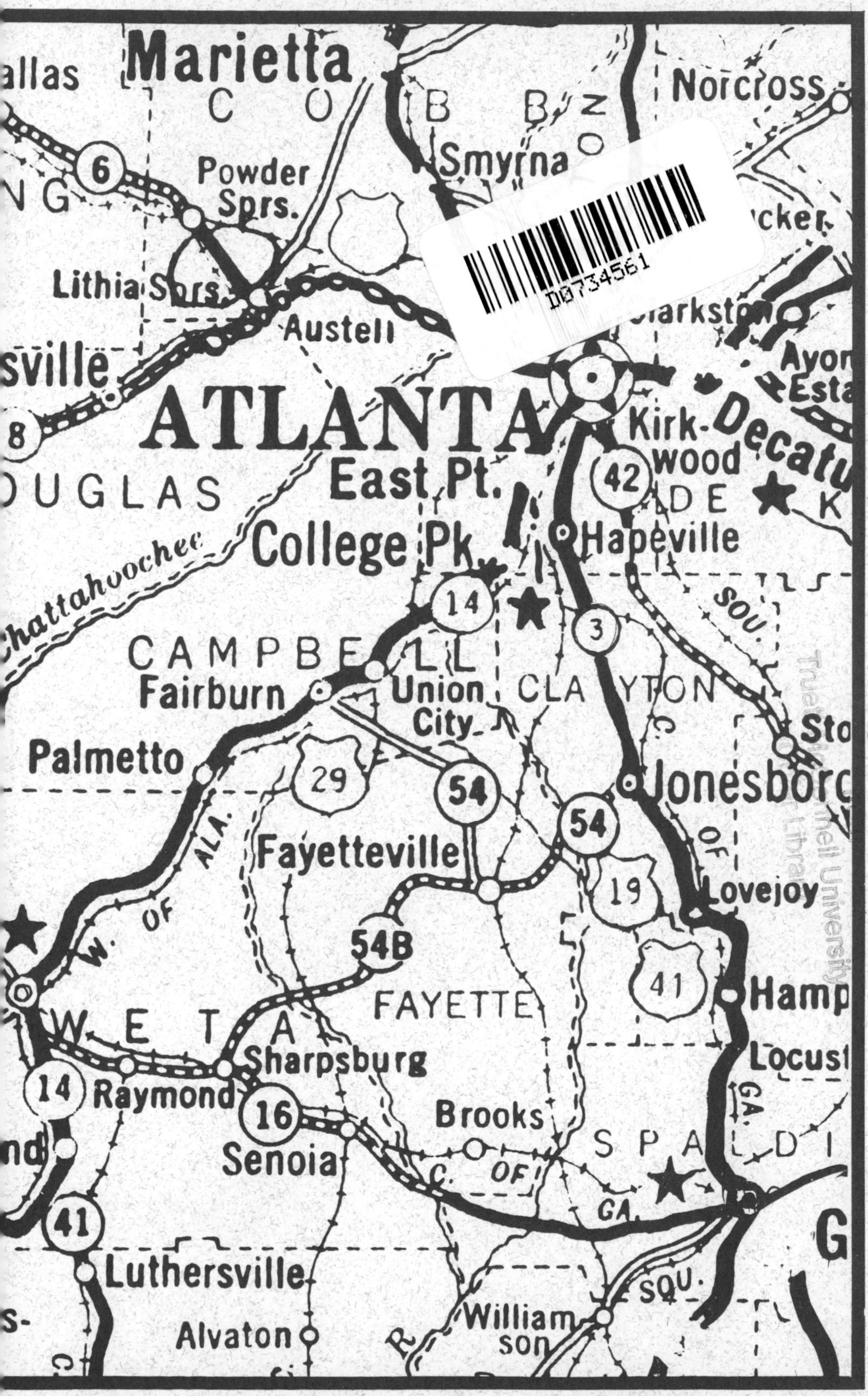

Georgia 1929

DILIGENT
IN HIS
BUSINESS

Warren Sewell

DILIGENT IN HIS BUSINESS: WARREN SEWELL

by

Edwin C. Godbold

Contents

Dedicated

To My Wife
Virginia Jones Godbold

Preface

This book is an account of the life and work of Warren Palmer Sewell, who was born in 1888 on a small farm in Alabama and became an exemplary salesman and a successful manufacturer of men's clothing, first in Atlanta, then in west Georgia.

He had a great deal to do with the establishment of the clothing industry in the South; indeed, the firms he began are running strong in the 1980s. Additionally, he founded a large and vigorous family, which has always been deeply involved in the clothing business and in civic and community affairs. These family successors are continuing in his trail as people of business accomplishment and citizens of responsible outlook and endeavor.

Warren Sewell was a deeply religious man who took a profound interest in his employees and in his neighbors. His story is that of a vibrant, busy, creative, and happy man.

The primary sources for this book are detailed personal interviews conducted during 1983 and 1984 by the author with more than a hundred people who knew Warren Sewell.

The people interviewed included, for example, his younger brother, one of his two wives, his three surviving children, a daughter-in-law, two sons-in-law, his grandchildren, various fishing companions, fellow farmers, his longtime chauffeur, church associates, his pastor, his attorney, his accountant, peer industrialists, bankers large and small, suppliers of cloth, competitors, schoolmates, neighbors, clothing store owners, and clothing manufacturers.

Warren Sewell Clothing Company employees, both active and retired, constituted an especially valuable source of information. They included salesmen, sewing-room supervisors, machine operators, maintenance men, designers, plant supervisors, stockroom workers, accountants and credit officials, pressing-room workers, designers, quality control supervisors—in sum, workers from the rag man and the wrinkle-knocker in the plant to the manufacturing superintendent and the chairman of the board.

The people interviewed were unfailingly helpful, and in spite of their diverse backgrounds and varying professions and viewpoints, they all possessed one sterling quality: they wanted to talk about Warren Sewell. And in doing so they made this book possible.

One or two interviews were by phone, and one was by correspondence, while all the rest were by face-to-face visits, frequently of long duration. Some people were interviewed more than once, one or two of them several times. Many not only talked but also provided clippings, letters, and photographs. These people contributed substantially to the book, and thanks go to them. They are listed in the notes on interviews.

Members of the Sewell family were communicative, open, and helpful. The family furnished the genealogical notes that appear in the back. Photographs on the following pages appear courtesy of the Georgia Department of Archives and History: 4-7, 12, 14-16, 21, 23-24, 26, 28-30, 32-34, 47, 50, 59, 62, 163, 177, 179, 204.

The staffs of two organizations were consistently helpful and accommodating—the Georgia Department of Archives and History and Mercer University Press.

The Warren and Ava Sewell Foundation generously supported this work. The Warren Sewell Clothing Company made available company records, photographs, and documents. Three company people in particular contributed to the progress of this book, assisting and smoothing the way all along—Lamar Plunkett, J. Mac Smith, and L. Richard Plunkett.

A special debt of gratitude is due to all my own family for support and encouragement, particularly to my wife, Virginia.

Edwin C. Godbold
August 1985
Atlanta, Georgia

Seest thou a man diligent
in his business?
He shall stand before kings.

Proverbs 22:29
King James Version

·CHAPTER I·

Beginnings

Warren Sewell was plowing the red soil of his father's east Alabama farm, walking behind a mule. It was the spring of 1905, and he found nothing new or strange in what he did. More than sixteen years old, sturdy and big-framed, Warren had started plowing the hard-scrabble land at age eight; then the plow handles sloping upward from the stock were cut down to a comfortable height, about waist high, to fit his size.

On this warm spring day he paused to watch a shining hack on the nearby country road wheeling along in the bright sunshine behind a spirited team of horses. At the reins was a man of commanding presence, a drummer, a traveling salesman—stiff white straw hat tilted on his head, cigar in his mouth, arm bands on the sleeves of his shirt—headed to show his wares in one town, then another.

Warren gazed until the driver, team, and hack were out of sight, his spirit and imagination suffused by what he saw and by the promise of it. Standing in a plowed field with the red dust on his rough shoes and the plow lines easy in his hands, he knew that day with clarity and conviction what he wanted to be and what he was determined to be: a salesman, free to go, to travel, to earn, to have a life relieved of poverty. It was, he said, a sensation so vivid and clear that it remained with him always.

The young Sewell standing bemused and exhilarated in the warm Alabama spring was a product of four generations of Sewells in the east Alabama and west Georgia area.

In 1806 his great-great-grandparents, John and Mary Sewell, left their home near Kannapolis in Rowan County, North Carolina, and followed several brothers and sisters to Franklin County, Georgia. Bringing with them their first child, one-year-old Elizabeth, John and Mary settled on 110 acres near the Grove fork of the Broad River. In 1807 their second child, a son, was born on this Georgia farm, to be followed by nine more children during the next seventeen years.

Among these children was Warren Sewell's greatgrandfather, John Asberry Sewell, the ninth child, born 10 January 1820. At nineteen he married fourteen-year-old Martha Polk, and with their two children they moved into Alabama, settling near Centre. In all, they had thirteen children. Martha died at age forty, and John Asberry married Hannah Morgan a year later, a widow with two children of her own. Together they had four sons and four daughters. The remarkable Hannah Morgan Sewell cared for ten children of her own and thirteen stepchildren, raising sixteen of the twenty-three to maturity.

Among the stepchildren was Levi Frances, Warren Sewell's grandfather, the first son of John Asberry. He was born 15 November 1840 at Erastus, Georgia, near Lavonia.

Levi served in the Confederate army, married Martha Frances Morgan, and eventually moved his family to Randolph County, Alabama, settling on eighty acres bought for eighty dollars. He farmed, bought more land, prospered, and was named justice of the peace. In addition, he operated a store at Graham, Alabama, and after a stay in Carrollton,

Georgia, settled in Bowdon, Georgia, where he invested in a bank and managed it.

His bank went under in the 1920s; he lost heavily, virtually all that he had. A grandniece recalls his coming to see her family in Graham, where he displayed the hole in his shoe and his worn, almost ragged clothing. He would live in Bowdon until age eighty-five.

The oldest of the six children of Levi and Martha was Warren Sewell's father, Willis Columbus, born 3 January 1867 in Roscoe, Coweta County, Georgia. He attended school in Big Springs and, according to a cousin who lived close by, took on early the duties of the eldest son, working hard on his father's farm. He married a neighbor's daughter, Willie Martha Frances Roseborough Gay, called Rose by her father, Willie by everyone else.

Willie, who grew up just after the Civil War, told her children that she "learned to write in the sand with a straw." She was raised by a stepmother who taught her household skills, including carding of cotton thread by hand, and use of the spinning wheel. Her domestic duties also entailed dyeing, along with weaving cloth for pants, sheets, and dresses on the hand loom.

Her father raised medicinal shrubs and herbs—horehound, comfrey, bugbane, heart leaves—and transmitted his lore to her. He kept a side saddle on the porch and a hitching block nearby, so that his wife and girls could mount and ride as they wished. Willie liked to ride. When she and Willis were courting, they frequently went by mule-back to neighborhood singings.

Willis and Willie set up housekeeping in a small house on his parents' Randolph County farm. When his father, Levi, moved to Carrollton, Georgia, Willis took over the farm and operated it.

To augment his farm earnings Willis worked for McConnell and Christopher—a wholesale general merchandise house of Atlanta—as a traveling salesman for dry goods, notions, and shoes. He loaded his trunks and sample cases into a hack, and with a driver handling a span of horses, he covered his sales territory. He arranged to be home on weekends, so he could join with his wife and the hired men in planning the next week's farm work. He spent most of his time on the road, drumming, and was viewed by most as more of a drummer than a farmer.

When a neighbor asked Willie Sewell about her first child, did she want a girl or a boy, she replied that she wanted a boy. "I thought you'd want a girl so she could help you cook and wash the dishes." Her response was, "I can cook and wash the dishes. I want a boy so I can send him to the mill to get me some meal."

The first child of Willie and Willis Sewell was born 29 October 1888, and they named him Warren Palmer. Willie gave Warren educational instruction before he began school. A lifelong acquaintance of Warren said that Warren told him a thousand times how his mother "first taught me how to

A small Georgia hack equipped as a store and filled with various wares that are advertised on the outside. Early 1900s.

*Two traveling salesmen in horse and buggy with small bag in the foot of the vehicle.
Calhoun County, Georgia, 1900.*

write in the sand in the yard''—just as her own mother had done for her.

In 1894 or 1895, when Warren was six or seven years old, his father sold the Alabama farm and moved his growing family to nearby Buchanan, Georgia, where he operated a general store in association with one of his brothers, James or Shelley, and with their father Levi.

After the family's arrival in Buchanan young Warren

Warren Sewell, 1889.

began his formal schooling, enrolling under Professor W. T. Daniel and continuing in this school during the family's stay of three or four years. On Warren's tenth birthday, 29 October 1898, the Sewell store in Buchanan and its merchandise burned. There was no insurance, and as Warren recounted, his father shortly "went down and bought a farm in Randolph County, Alabama, for cash money furnished by our grandfather." The loan at eight percent took Willis years to repay, especially when their single cash crop, cotton, brought only seven cents a pound.

Warren described the 480-acre Alabama farm as "rough, undeveloped land," explaining that the house had to be renovated "where we could live in it" and that they needed to reclaim much bottom land—on the flood plain of a stream, heavily timbered and dense with undergrowth and vines.

In these circumstances ten-year-old Warren in late 1898 or early 1899 began helping in earnest with the farm work. "I was the oldest child, with five brothers and sisters younger than I was, and with other children coming along constantly." His brother Roy commented, "Warren, the first born, accepted the responsibility of his place in the family and became our mother's right arm. Our father was traveling

Middle of Main Street, Bowdon, Georgia, 1897.

W. D. Lovvorn's store, Newell, Alabama, near Graham, early 1900s.

nearly every week and Warren undertook the duties of farm manager."

Plowing since he was eight, Warren knew how to back the plow out at the end of a row; understood why the cows had to be kept out of the bitterweed in early spring; could split shingles with a froe and a maul; and was accustomed to picking cockleburs out of the hair of dogs and the tails of mules.

He knew these country things, and he would learn more through his constant farm work, month after month, for years to come. Each spring in placid rhythm he would take the steps to prepare the land for plowing: clear the briers and bushes from the fence corners, ditch the banks, chop down and burn the dried cornstalks from the previous crop. Then he would plow, plant, and cultivate in order eventually to reap and store.

In 1900 Willis and Willie Sewell were living on their Graham, Alabama, farm, which contained fields, pasture, barn, cow lot, wood lot, garden, cane mill, arbor—the altogether practical equipment that made the farm virtually self-sufficient. The farmhouse itself, sitting on the edge of their land and within sight of the road from Bowdon, had a shady porch that occupied the front and two sides. It was a big and rambling house with four bedrooms, each with two beds. As Warren's younger brother Roy recalled, "We were a big family in a big house, every bed filled." He and Warren slept "in the side room, just off the kitchen."

When the census-taker stopped at the house in 1900, there were six children, ranging in age from twelve to two. The three boys were Warren, twelve; Robert, nine; and Roy, two. The three girls were Lura May, eight; Martha Frances, five; and Lois, four. Within three years there would be two more children, both boys: Carl Gay, born in November 1900, and Byrd, born in May 1903. There were three children who died in infancy—Amos in 1890, Floy in 1902, and Eva in 1909.

Their father, Willis Sewell, was a genial man of great friendliness. A farm neighbor, a cousin to Willis, said of him, "He was a great hand to visit. He would get in the buggy and come to our house and spend the day and talk and just sit around the fire."

Willis's physical actions and work capacity were inhibited by physical disability. While he was tall and big-framed, a splendid figure of a man, he suffered from diabetes, for which there was no effective treatment. Prey to a love of good food and eating, he did not know how to care for his ailment. As a result he was a tremendous man, "the biggest man in girth I ever saw," commented one neighbor. Willis weighed about 325 pounds and wore a size 60 or 62 suit. A clothing plant employee who cut him a suit said that even when Willis had been ill and lost weight, he still took a size 56-stout.

A cousin recounted that when Willis shifted from horse-drawn travel he drove "a little old Model T roadster with one of those little old turtle backs on it." However, because of his size he sat not behind the steering wheel but to the side of it.

His children knew that his being ill and overweight bothered him, even depressed him. One commented: "He never got any encouragement out of this world." Despite his size and the deceptive congeniality that covered his worries,

The Sewells' Graham, Alabama, home.

Willis Columbus Sewell, Warren's father.

he was a worker. Said an aged sharecropper who spent twelve years on the Sewells' Graham farm: "Mr. Willis was a big man, couldn't see his feet. He'd get in the field and get that mule a-going, when it was too hot to work, the water and sweat a-gushin' from him. He loved to go, he sho' did. He was a good worker." A relative and neighbor characterized Willis as "a minute man, who didn't have time, always in a hurry," adding that his father Levi was that way too, as was his son Warren.

Will Roop, who started in the retail grocery business in Bowdon in 1912, knew Willis well and for a long time. He said:

> He was a traveling man, a great guy. His boys came to it naturally. He traveled this whole territory—a big old hack with big trunks on it. All the little towns in those days had showrooms where salesmen could open up their trunks and display their goods. Merchants would go in and buy from them.

But Willis did not have the knack of making money. As a

businessman and salesman, he was more widely known and respected for his companionable nature than for any unusual success. He was not inclined to play hunches or take chances, and if a substantial selling or business opportunity came his way, he invariably missed it. However, he was a steadfast and good salesman, and his sons Warren, Robert, and Roy inherited the selling knack from him and were blessed to do so.

Willis's wife, Willie, was a woman of great energy and strength of moral purpose. She had traits of character that helped to make life in the Sewell household lively and spirited as well as controlled and efficient. There were duties she devised for the children; yet while insisting on home industries and productive work for them, Willie found time to encourage both cultural pursuits and their studies.

She loved good books, and so urged her children to read, especially aloud, and to help each other with their lessons. She sponsored spelling matches and frequent math drills for them. She played the accordion, led the family in singing, and was fond of music and dancing. She could quote poetry and long passages from the Bible. She "made the Bible truths her own," as her son Roy put it, and for every emergency she had a proverb or biblical saying such as:

> *Eat not the bread of idleness.*
> *Be ye kind.*
> *If you make your bed hard, turn over oftener.*
> *A good name is rather to be chosen than great riches.*
> *Hold your head up even if you die hard.*
> *What can't be cured must be endured.*
> *Buy truth and sell it not.*

She had a strong personality and could be firmly hardheaded. Once her husband Willis thought he would sell the farm and head west. He found a buyer and arranged a deal. But she refused to sign the deed, even when one of the interested parties heatedly shook his walking stick in her face.

Her capacity for work was amazing. She arose early to grind coffee beans, knead out biscuit dough, fill pitchers with

Two Georgia traveling salesmen, early 1900s.
Abe Ellis (left) peddled beef and Reuben Smith sold Tip-Top bread.

ribbon cane syrup, pour buttermilk, and fry ham or bacon. She cooked for them all, including the fieldworking convicts her husband sometimes employed, as did other farmers.

Her kitchen was the center of the family life, with its large wood-burning stove, dining table, flour and corn meal containers, and fireplace.

At night she sewed for the family and the hired help and knitted the numerous socks needed by her children. She used a small brass lamp to supplement the regular kerosene lamp and the firelight.

Most observers saw Willie as what one of them termed "the big bee of the family." In the quietness of a plain and not wealthy rural life, she nonetheless brought her children many amenities. She not only managed, she also made the home a hospitable place. Preachers, peddlers, and salesmen were welcome to food and, if night overtook them on the road, to lodging.

Clyde (Buck) Newell, Warren Sewell's black chauffeur for many years, recollected with delight Willie Sewell's open-handed hospitality whenever he stepped into their bright kitchen with the fireplace in it: "You walk in her house, you got to eat—breakfast, lunch, supper, too, three meals every day you're there. She'd say, 'what you want, coffee, ice tea, buttermilk, sweet milk?' " Though the family was not wealthy, their table was attractive and the food abundant and appetizing.

The Sewell parents were Primitive Baptists, faithful members of the Shiloh Baptist Church in Graham. As their son Roy put it, his parents were "loyal to their faith, never tiring of good works." He remembers them as gay and happy people, though on Sunday all work and even play was stopped. "Our sisters were not even allowed to press a garment on Sunday." All the family went to Sunday school and regular church service without fail.

The couple saw to it that the children had the chance to learn from the example they set for them. The clerk of the Shiloh Baptist Church commented that Willis was the cleanest man in speech he ever knew. A salesman acquaintance said that Willis, "as well as the mother, taught the boys that God came first in their lives."

The parents' attention to these matters and their own living examples resulted in indelible impressions on their children. An Atlanta banker said of Warren that he "had some great basics engrained in him by his parents. He was a fundamentalist in his spiritual roots. He worked hard, was in-

Willie Gay Sewell, Warren's mother.

telligent, wrote a fine hand, looked like he had a lot of penmanship as a boy."

The family was active in the affairs of the community, ready to join in neighborhood social events—to celebrate birthdays, to help with church dinners on the grounds, to go to a log rolling, to assist in raising a barn, to lend a helping hand with the sick.

The Sewells were independent people. Neither of the parents had any patience with people who would not work for themselves. The virtues of work were instilled in their children early, "from the start," commented a neighbor. They were a family particularly set on demonstrating their integrity.

Willie's son Roy said they were as rural a family as could be, describing them as "close knit and loyal. I suppose we took our cue from our parents who were devoted to each other and gave their love equally to all of us." He felt that whatever good qualities he might have acquired were developed in that household. When asked what single thing contributed most to his brother Warren's success, Roy instantly

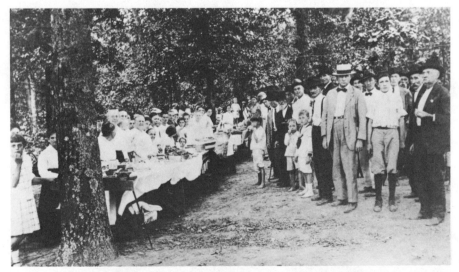

Dinner on the grounds, Tallapoosa Primitive Baptist Church,
Tyus Road, Carroll County, about 1910.

Bowdon, Georgia, about 1900.
At the left Postmaster Joe Walker stands in front of the post office.

responded: "Probably our mother—her love and prayers. That's where I drew my strength, too."

After the time of the 1900 census life for the Sewell clan continued in normal country fashion for a few years. Willis managed to maintain a precarious balance between farming and selling on the road; he made small but regular payments on the debt to his father for the farm purchase. Three more children were born (in late 1900, in 1902, and in 1903), with two of them, both boys, surviving.

Working the land had been a family tradition for generations, and Warren was raised to follow the plow like his father. Warren persisted at farm work to assist his father. In the midst of this life in Graham, Warren secured some schooling for himself. The other children continued school or, as they grew to the right age, commenced school.

By the spring of 1905 Warren, who was sixteen, had for six years been heavily committed to farm work and to the responsibilities of the oldest child in a busy household where the father was most often away.

Warren bound himself to the farm and its labor and made sure that the younger children had every possible benefit of schooling. In the spring of 1905 he had stood transfigured in the fresh-plowed soil at the vision of himself as a free traveler and a salesman. His belief in this hope made him restless about his future. A friend and associate of Warren for years, Raymond Otwell, commented that Warren sometimes spoke of his 1905 resolution to become a salesman, telling him that he knew then "that's what I want to be. There never was any doubt."

The spirit and understanding with which Warren served as his mother's right arm may be measured by the 1983 comment of his brother Roy: "Warren was father, mother and older brother to me."

Warren and Robert, the two older brothers, worked in harmony on the farm. Robert was three years younger and was the dreamer, the imaginative one, with Warren seeming by comparison more self-controlled and solid. Said Roy, "They made a perfect team as far as family life was con-

Buchanan Street, Bremen, Georgia, 1910—
an unpaved street with a well in the center.

cerned." Gay and Roy, twelve and eight years younger than
Warren, were more of the same age and were close companions, sharing work and play on the farm.

Cooperation and mutual effort were key elements in the
Sewell home and on the farm. Nephew Ray Sewell said of his
uncles that all were dedicated to their mother Willie and her
welfare and to their home. "Their mother skilled them in—
and they were very strong in—a real concern about their
whole family and their whole family's welfare." He added
that they had a keen sense that each child had a responsibility to the whole family, not just for being personally successful, "but for remaining always dedicated to and responsible
for every other family member." The result was, as another
observer put it, "a family of strong-minded people who saw
that the family never wanted."

It was natural, though, that there was competition as well
as cooperation. When the children took their sacks and went
to the field to pick cotton, they measured their achievements
against each other. In this event and elsewhere it was a race
for accomplishment, for contribution, for recognition. And
not only did one have to compete, one had to do well. A close
observer of the Willis Sewell clan said: "When Sewells are
ploughing and one runs a furrow that isn't straight, they all
get into a fight."

For Warren—the oldest child, the family leader—striv-
ing for position and maintaining it meant much to him. While
young, he determined that within the family and elsewhere
in life he would not take second place. His zeal for work was
matched by an earnest and quiet conviction that he was and
should be first, and best. The achieved result was a powerful
combination—his vision of himself as a salesman and his
unease at ever being in second place.

In the fall of 1906, when Warren would reach age eighteen, his father told him he would never be able to send him
to college "because I have too many other children to look
after." But he added that if Warren wanted to attend school
in Bowdon, he could do so—"after we get our cotton picked
and get through in the field." Warren could then remain at

Willis and Willie Sewell in front of the Graham home,
surrounded by their children—in all, seven boys and four girls—and visitors.

school until cotton planting the next spring, around 20-25 April.

This kind of schedule was a variation on the long-standing calendar of Bowdon College, which from its first days had attempted to conform to the financial and family needs of the students. The fall term began the second week in August, after crops had been laid by. At the end of October the long Christmas vacation began, lasting until January of the next year. Students dispersed to their homes to help gather fall crops. The second term began the second week in January and continued until the first week in July, though there was a long vacation in May, so that the boys could help with spring planting.

Warren was ready for school, both to free himself from the drudgery of farm life and to further his goal of becoming a salesman. He had thought much about being a physician, because he believed, as he told his daughter Charlotte, that medicine was "God's greatest calling." He had attempted unsuccessfully to borrow money from his thrifty grandfather for his medical education. He now knew that he had neither the money nor the background for medicine, thus he yearned for and was ready to go to Bowdon College.

After fodder-pulling time in the fall of 1906 Warren and a sister went to Bowdon College in Graham as boarding students. He roomed with the J. B. Fowler family, just across the street from the college. Warren had no income of any kind, but a college official he described as "a very good man teacher, W. P. Lunceford," got him a job to earn his board and a little spending money. Warren's description of his benefactor perhaps indicates the small size and informal nature of the college; Lunceford was president of the college at the time and remained so until 1908.

Warren and a student friend, Joe Morris, did the janitorial work in the school, including sweeping the floors and lighting a small boiler each morning. For their labors they were paid fifty cents a day.

Bowdon College, Bowdon, Georgia.

When Warren began at Bowdon College, most of the faculty were preachers. There was only one woman professor.

Chapel services were held each morning, and both teachers and students were required to attend. Students answered chapel roll call with a biblical verse. Some of the boys always responded with the same verse; the girls prided themselves on offering a different one each day.

Warren was in the eighth grade when he began and in this initial year he finished that grade and part of the ninth.

He belonged to the boys' Clay and Calhoun Society, which met each week and provided practice in public speaking, debating, and declamation. Another Bowdon College student said Warren excelled at speaking and "was a persuasive talker, as were all the Sewells." For the girls there was the Clioman Society. Its weekly programs consisted of readings, essays, recitations, debates, and vocal and instrumental music.

A fellow student of Warren said that her studies consisted of Latin, mathematics, algebra, elocution, English, and

Student body, Bowdon College, early 1900s.

composition and rhetoric. Warren's must have been similar. She said that at first Warren lagged in some subjects, from inadequate background preparation in his earlier schooling, "not from lack of application." He soon overcame these shortcomings and was a brilliant student, doing well in all subjects, especially mathematics, and was on the honor roll for those averaging in the 90s.

Once, when she was on the honor roll along with her two girl cousins, Warren was also, as the only boy. The college was very strict and had few social activities. However, the honor students were allowed to walk uptown and look in the store windows. As their honor group strolled to town, Warren wondered aloud why he, who did so well in mathematics, did not perform as well in Latin as she did. She said she gave him two reasons, neither of which he liked and both of which made him scuff his heels as he walked along: girls are smarter than boys, and she had had a private tutor since she was twelve.

She was glad that Warren went into the clothing business, because as a boy in school his trousers were so short they came up above the top of his high-button shoes, "and you could see his socks."

Warren's account of the end of the school year in the spring of 1907 had a wistful note to it. He reported that he left school "before any of the commencement exercises or anything was planned and went back home," to farm and home duties.

In his second year Warren—who was nineteen in the fall of 1907—repeated his work-school procedure. He completed the ninth grade and part of the tenth, then "left school the latter part of April [1908] to plant cotton," to be reunited with the family, and to report his progress.

In 1908 after the summer's work was over the pattern again resumed—off to Bowdon College in the fall, where he turned twenty in late October. This year, though, there was a change. About Christmas time his father, who was taking one of Warren's cousins to Atlanta for a job interview,

Graduation Day, Bowdon College.

brought Warren along. This was Warren's first trip to Atlanta.

Willis called on a longtime acquaintance, S. F. McConnell, head of McConnell and Christopher Dry Goods Company, a leading general merchandise wholesale house for which Willis had traveled. McConnell was impressed with Warren, declined to employ the cousin, and offered Warren a job as a salesman, which would include receiving a hack, a pair of horses, and twenty-five dollars a week expense money. Warren was to care for and grease the hack, curry the horses, and feed and house the animals and himself on this budget. McConnell was cautious about advancing a country greenhorn twenty-five dollars for expenses. Warren's father agreed to the suggestion that if Warren did not make that amount during the year he would reimburse the firm for the advance.

His father decided to let Warren stay in Atlanta and take the job, while he returned to Graham to explain to Warren's mother. She was happy about the employment but dis-

A business day at a Georgia livery and feed stable, about 1900.

tressed at his taking Warren out of college and starting him in a brand new job "with only one clean shirt along."

From the fall of 1906 through the spring of 1908, over two bobtailed terms, Warren had rounded off the eighth grade, finished the ninth and part of the tenth. He probably completed the final portion of the tenth during his last fall there, in 1908. His sudden, mid-year departure was the last of formal schooling for him. Later in Atlanta he would work at a home-study course in business and thereafter always read widely and intensively, but Bowdon College's tenth grade was his last regularized study.

Warren had been eager to attend Bowdon College and had used the hard-earned time to his advantage. However, he never forgot his vision and commitment to a life of travel and selling. As he left Bowdon College he exchanged compulsory chapel, Latin, and janitorial duties, and the Clay and Calhoun Society for the open road, the north Georgia mountains, and life as a traveling salesman.

His formal schooling behind him, Warren took over his hack, the two horses, and the trunks containing dry goods and notions—which he explained were "any little thing that women buy in a country store." He also had his suitcase, the necessary supply of clean shirts from his mother, and the optimism of one who has attained an initial goal.

Around the first of January, 1909 he headed out of Atlanta into his territory—the middle part of north Georgia, from Atlanta up to the mountains. McConnell had told him that any time he heard a train whistle blow, he should turn in the other direction, for he was out of his territory.

At age twenty Warren was at last, as he put it, "a real dirt drummer." And he gloried in the work. He told how he lived in the country, spending the night with merchants or farmers, "and got the best training a boy ever had. It was a great opportunity." At the end of the selling year he left his hack and a pair of horses in Carrollton and went home to Graham for his twenty-first birthday, having earned not only the expense advance but also a check for $375. When he gave the check to his father, the two of them went to the Bradley

Stone's General Store, Jasper County, Georgia, 1913.
Teams standing outside where a checker game is underway.

and Hyatt store in Carrollton and cashed it. His father persuaded Warren to take twenty-five dollars, telling him he
wished he could give him "what a worthy son should have
to start life with."

After his birthday festivities at home Warren returned to
Atlanta. The no-railroad territory he had been assigned was
not especially promising, and some of his customers had told
him that the goods he was selling were not as desirable as
those of some of his competitors. His customers were beginning to buy from another concern with a larger line and a better selection. These reactions from the marketplace were
important to him. He was, he said, "a young fellow naturally
looking for a better proposition."

So at five o'clock one afternoon he went to the competing firm, Reagan and Malone, a leading Atlanta wholesale
house, and asked Reagan for a selling job. Reagan did not try
to hide his opinion that Warren probably had no ability at all.
His response to the request for a job was, "How many goods

can you sell—75 or 50 cents worth?" Warren told him of his past-year sales, but Reagan told him "a boy won't do." Warren recounted, "When Mr. Reagan told me I couldn't do it, I got insulted and said, 'Well, it's all right.' So I just went on out."

At seven the next morning Warren was walking to the Atlanta railroad station, expecting to catch a train to Carrollton, get his hack, and resume his drumming. A message from Reagan asked Warren to see him, which he did. Either a night's reflection or a check on Warren had changed Reagan, for Warren found "an entirely different man," who offered him a job and a pair of matched grey mules to drive. The team was waiting north of Atlanta in Woodstock, Georgia. All this amounted to no small offer. Perhaps still rankled from the past conversation, Warren refused, saying he was not traveling any more out of Atlanta by driving mules or horses; however, he would ride the train and then either hire people to haul him where he wanted to go or rent a temporary rig for himself.

They talked along and settled on Warren's travel method, fifty dollars a month starting salary, a commission if he sold more than that, and a territory from Marietta to Copperhill, Tennessee, along the L & N Railroad and up the Southern from Atlanta to Cornelia and north to Franklin, North Carolina.

Reagan, getting in the last word, told Warren that if he did not make good, "I'll fire you. I'll not give you any alternative." Later Warren found some satisfaction in the fact that Reagan, with his salesman traveling by train, had to sell the pair of grey mules in Woodstock.

It was early November 1909 when Warren went directly off to work for Reagan and Malone. No one said what happened to the horses and hack Warren left in Carrollton. If the farm boy ever had any callowness or self-doubt, it was gone now. Determined pursuit of his goal had toughened his morale.

A buggy pulled by a matched pair of Georgia mules, about 1900.

Roy felt that his brother's move from hack to train travel was a real advance. "Now Warren was a big city boy, bought his ticket and shipped his trunk wherever he was going."

For one of his reasonably close sales areas, Warren rode the train from Atlanta to Chamblee. Here he called on Wallace and Warnock, a general-merchandise company, feed store, and livery stable, selling them work pants. He would buy a sack of feed, rent a horse and buggy, and take off for Alpharetta, Dawsonville, Emma, Ball Ground, and points north. In a week he would return, pay for the horse and buggy, and catch the train back into Atlanta. For longer-distance travel he generally rode the train and then hired a driver and team at his destination.

At year's end when Warren went to keep his twenty-second birthday date at home, he carried along his commission check for $1,350, the top amount paid to any of the firm's twelve salesmen. He asked his mother's recommendation on use of the money, and perhaps recollecting the family's disastrous Buchanan fire, she suggested that he buy land: "It

Carrollton, Georgia, livery stable, Alabama Street, 1905.

might wash away, but it won't burn up, and you'll always have a home." He invested in land, "pasture and pine," as he described it. Many years later at age eighty-four he proudly said he still owned it. One wonders how many times in the intervening sixty-three years he walked through that pasture land and among those pines, putting his hand on their rough brown bark and remembering how he earned them.

His brother Roy reminisced about the Warren of this period: "Warren continued to sell. Yes, Warren grew up, he did, and my daddy had great pride in him, and my mother." As he matured, his love for selling and for the life of a salesman grew. He entered every general store and dry-goods store with enthusiasm and pleasure, along with an intent to sell. He was at home at the sight of the shelves filled with yard goods—printed cotton, bleached linen, worsted, tweed.

Warren worked with Reagan and Malone for three years, until some time in 1912 or 1913, when he left the firm because a territory he desired and felt he had been promised was given

Ten groomed bay horses in front of a north Georgia livery stable,
Logan's, on Park Avenue, Calhoun, 1914.

to another salesman. He said, "Immediately I started looking
for another job. I was never satisfied not to keep making
progress." He went up the street to A. M. Robinson Dry
Goods Company, another leading firm, and became a salesman for them. Here he met J. D. Robinson, who would succeed his father as head of this firm and eventually move into
the First National Bank, where he and Warren would continue their personal and business relationship.

After three years with Robinson Warren shifted over in
1915 or 1916 to John E. Hurst, a Baltimore wholesale dry-
goods house. They hired him for $200 a month and ex-
penses, giving him the territory from Atlanta to Athens on
the Seaboard Railway and from Atlanta to Greenville, South
Carolina, on the Southern. He was to remain with the Hurst
firm until early 1921. Warren explained, "I had no problems,
just worked right on and made considerably more money."

Robert Sewell, three years younger than Warren, went
to Bowdon College, then on to a boarding school at Cave

Interior of a small-town general store, Georgia, early 1900s.

Springs, Georgia. When a smallpox scare led him to believe the school would be quarantined, he ran away and persuaded Warren to help him get a traveling job. Warren explained, "I had a brother, Robert, who was a great brother, and I wanted to see him get along too. And he got a job traveling and did all right."

Roy recounts that when Warren shifted from horse and mule to train travel, Robert "succeeded Warren in the hack and then traveled out of Atlanta on the train for John Silvey Company." Robert married in 1918.

Both Warren and Robert enjoyed the prosperity of the boom years of World War I and after, when cotton sold for as much as forty-two cents a pound. They worked hard, represented two top-flight wholesale dry-goods houses, made money, and saved it.

As an aside to their dry-goods traveling, they had a small personal operation: jobbing men's wear, overcoats, trousers, and now and then a suit. They developed a plan for an expanded jobbing business in men's pants to be conducted along with their traveling jobs. George Longino explained

Teachers and their elementary and high school students,
Hamilton College, Bremen, Georgia, about 1905.

that "they wanted an operation where goods could be shipped in to them and they could go out and sell, coming in on the weekends to ship them out." They felt they could successfully merge the two selling operations and give their weekend time to the pants business. They arranged to buy pants from a New York manufacturer.

Their younger brother Roy joined them in Atlanta. After attending country schools at Graham, Comer, and Newell and Bowdon College, he graduated from London High School and in 1918 entered Alabama Polytechnic Institute in Auburn, Alabama. Like Warren, Roy had aspirations to be a doctor, but his school preparation was inadequate. By Thanksgiving 1919 of his second year at Auburn he knew he was going to fail if he returned after the Thanksgiving vacation. He told his circumstances to his brother Warren in Atlanta, who agreed to give him a job.

Roy, who was twenty-one, worked in the Sewells' Mitchell Street jobbing office, "shipped the goods, swept the floors, and with the help of a secretary ran the office." His two brothers, traveling by railroad and in "two old Buicks, later Fords," were there on the weekends to help make up the orders. Of the jobbing operation, Roy said: "Anyone other than my brother Warren would have gone broke." Roy undertook his work with enthusiasm and vigor, and they soon put him on the road. "I wasn't the best salesman in the world," noted Roy, "but I was pretty good."

Robert, always a great salesman, could spot an opportunity from afar. Said Roy: "About this time Robert went down to Roanoke, Alabama, and bought overalls at $6 a dozen and sold them for $10—overalls! I guarantee you he was a man who was going to do it some way."

In seeking an office for their expanded jobbing business, Robert, who lived in College Park, told their plans to George Longino, cashier of the Bank of College Park; he was also affiliated with a bank in Fairburn. Longino became interested in the enterprise, with the result that in the spring of 1921 he, Warren, and Robert each put in $10,000 and formed a part-

A Georgia traveling salesman and his Model T Ford, 1928.

*Georgia traveling salesman standing by his automobile, displaying products
(flavorings and seasonings) to a prospective customer, 1916.*

nership, the Sewell-Longino Company. Warren commented
that his wife and Robert's had been saving and were instrumental in their being able to go into the new business.

The vacant second floor of the Bank of College Park became headquarters for the new firm. While the Sewell brothers were out each week selling dry goods and pants, Longino
in his spare time worked as office manager, passed on credit
applications, and did the billing. When the brothers came in
on weekends, they all pitched in to pack and ship the week's
orders. From the beginning the business was good and the
firm was making money.

On the lookout to expand, they arranged to operate an
overcoat jobbing business for a New York firm. But with the
end of World War I and the readjustment of business to
peacetime conditions, the country suddenly found itself in a
depression. During one year cotton dropped from forty-two
cents a pound to ten cents. Merchants found themselves with

Robert and Josephine Sewell.

heavy inventories and with accounts receivable that were frozen. Banks were failing, and money was in short supply.

Just about the time the Sewells had overcoats spilling out the windows of their warehouse, the hard times hit. Warren said, "At the end of the year the bottom fell out. That was in 1921 and nobody could do anything." However, they were able to return the unsold stock of overcoats to the New York manufacturer, Sam Finkelstein, without penalty or loss. An unsellable inventory then would have collapsed their operations.

Warren took a look at the affairs of the jobbing venture, found they owed $125,000 and had accounts receivable of $130,000. He termed the receivables "chips and whet-stones," meaning many little accounts from small store-keepers around the Southeast, all of whom were caught in the depression.

It was a disheartening situation. "In effect," said Longino, "they were broke and had no more funds to put in the

business." Warren and Robert felt prompt action was necessary if they were to save the business. They boarded the
train to New York to see their creditors, carrying baskets of
food prepared by their wives for their dinner and supper. At
Richmond they shifted from the day coach to the pullman,
and in New York they stayed in the cheapest hotel they could
find.

They had only three substantial creditors—"thank
goodness for that," said Warren—and to each of them they
owed about $35,000. They called first on one of their sup-
pliers, Harry Berken, telling him that everybody in the
Southeast was broke, and going out of business, but that they
wanted a chance to continue to operate and pay their debts.
They felt capable of doing this, given reasonable time.

When Berken asked what they wanted him to do, Warren said they wanted notes for thirty, sixty, and ninety days.
Berken replied, "No. There's a depression. You can't do it,
there ain't any way you can do it. Why in the hell don't you
ask for something you can pay?" He would charge them no
interest and suggested that they try to pay the debt off in
twelve months. On the spot he offered a single note for
$30,000 due in thirty days. Each month they were to pay him
what they could and issue a new note for the balance.

They agreed, and their second creditor, a larger firm with
more resources, not only fell in line with the same note arrangement but also continued to sell them goods. The third
firm behaved similarly. There was only one bank involved,
the Atlanta National, which Longino had earlier talked into
lending them a substantial amount. When the large merchandise creditors in New York agreed to go along, so did the
Atlanta bank.

Temporarily they were saved, impressed with their luck
and with being befriended and helped by the Jewish merchants in New York.

The overcoat scare and the ballooning debt concerned
Longino, who felt that if his bank employers in Atlanta
learned of the amount of debt the jobbing firm owed, the bank
would "lock us up before you say scat." He thought the part-

nership was going broke and wanted out. In early 1922 he sold his one-third interest to Warren and Robert for $2,500, $200 a month. They never missed a payment. "It was the best bargain anybody ever got," said Longino's son, noting that his father "went back to banking and industry and stayed there" and never had any sour grapes about the matter.

According to Warren, "We did not fail and nobody closed us out, but we were broke to beat the band." However, Roy said they were paying out so much, "you thought you never saw a company going broke so fast, but we were making money and putting it back in."

The account with the Atlanta National Bank remained open, as did their credit with the New York merchandisers. Both factors were helpful to them for temporary salvation and for the long-term task of working out of their hole. Once almost stranded financially, their hopes were now renewed and their purpose strong.

Roy noted that in the early days when "failure was peering in through the window," it was Warren's fearlessness that kept the business alive. He said Warren was a success from the start and termed him "honest, courageous, friendly and generous."

The business lessons in these events were not lost on Warren. He pointed out that if instead of only three large creditors there had been a number of smaller ones, they would have descended on the little firm and forced them into bankruptcy. As it was, their indebtedness was concentrated with a few men of high business intelligence who could appreciate their situation and thus allowed them time. From that day, he said, he was careful to concentrate his debt in as few hands as possible.

The disturbing recent events also developed his views on indebtedness, for he commented: "Well, debt is all right providing you have the opportunity to pay back. The greatest thing a man ever had is credit. I am more jealous of my credit than anything I ever had." Additionally, Warren was forthright in recognizing that the sympathetic attention and consideration offered by the Jewish merchants of New York were primary factors in giving him a chance to survive.

When George Longino sold his interest in the Sewell-Longino Company in 1922 to Warren and Robert, they admitted to partnership their youngest brother, Roy. "We started," recounted Warren, "just Robert and myself and a younger brother, Roy. He had no capital, but he worked, and that is all we wanted." A traveling salesman like the other two brothers, Roy was married on 25 June 1923.

What of Warren's personal life during these "dirt drummer" and jobbing years after he left Bowdon College in 1908? Over in Graham his father now primarily farmed. "He quit the road when the boys left home," said a neighbor and clothing salesman. Warren kept in close touch with the family, visiting Graham frequently or stopping by during his selling trips. He continued to assist and support all the family, insuring that his sisters, as well as the brothers so inclined, went to college.

Roy Sewell.

When Warren headed out of Atlanta each week to his rural north Georgia sales territory, he passed through Woodstock, a town of 442 residents in the southern part of Cherokee County, twelve miles south of Canton. Incorporated in 1879 by a legislative act that prohibited forever the sale of liquor within its bounds, Woodstock was on the rail line from Marietta to Canton. Forming the heart of a splendid agricultural district, it was within the north Georgia gold-mining area, and had supplies of mica and kaolin nearby. The abundance of water power on the nearby Little River and Noonday Creek insured the location in Woodstock of wool-carding and yarn-spinning plants. It was also the center of the largest mule auctioning and mule trading activity in the state.

When Warren traveled, he called on the dry-goods merchants in Woodstock, including N. A. Fowler, who ran a general merchandise store and who earlier had been elected the first mayor of Woodstock. On 19 June 1912, two and a half years after he left Graham, Warren, twenty-three, married the Fowlers' daughter, Ava Lee, twenty-four. Ava went to school in Woodstock and attended Bessie Tift College, where she majored in music.

Warren was the oldest of his family, Ava the youngest of hers and the last child remaining at home. Her parents were reluctant for her to leave them. Though they did not oppose the marriage, they asked that the young couple remain with them during their lives, staying with them in the Woodstock home. Warren and Ava agreed, moving in with her parents in the large frame house fronting the railroad and the highway.

Ava was already a member of the Woodstock Baptist Church, which had originally been Enon Baptist Church, founded in 1837. On 20 October 1912, four months after his marriage, Warren joined the Woodstock Baptist Church by transferring his membership from the Sewell family's Shiloh Baptist Church. J. M. Spinks was the Woodstock pastor, overseeing a membership of 125.

Seven months after he joined Ava's church it burned— on 4 May 1913. Four days after the loss the church appointed

Wedding day, 19 June 1912.
Ava Lee Fowler and Warren Sewell.

a building committee, and a week later in a meeting in the
local Methodist church the Woodstock Baptists selected a
committee of church members to solicit subscriptions for a
new building. Warren Sewell was named to the solicitation
committee, and the group added him also to the earlier-
selected building committee.

Some indication of his work on the new building was his
appointment nine months later, 14 February 1914, to a committee to write letters of thanks to contributors to the building fund who were not members. The replacement church
was a long time in construction, but was finally dedicated 19
August 1917, when Ava and Warren were still members in
Woodstock though they had moved to Atlanta. His name is
on the cornerstone with other building committee members,
including Ava's father.

In the fall of October 1915 Warren was placed on the
church finance committee, and in July 1916 he was on a panel
to arrange a protracted meeting for the preachers in the next

month. During the same year he was superintendent of the 115-member Sunday school. On 21 February of the following year, 1917, the Woodstock congregation elected him a deacon, and three months later he was ordained by his pastor, C. W. Henderson, who was assisted by visiting ministers and the church deacons.

Ava was as energetic in church duties as was Warren. In 1916 she assisted Pastor George Carroll to organize the young people's union. She also aided in writing the memorial for a deceased member. For a long time she was secretary of the Women's Missionary Union, keeping the records in a fine flowing hand. However, beginning in February 1912, four months before her marriage, she began a nine-month break in these secretarial duties and did not resume them until 14 November 1914, when she started signing the minutes as "Mrs. Ava Sewell."

Ava's father was a merchant, "a straight sort of a fellow," said one of his grandchildren. When he ate a peppermint in the store, he put a penny in the cash register so his partner would not be cheated. Life with Ava's parents in some ways constrained the young couple. Warren even bought half the parents' Woodstock home to create a partial feeling of independence.

After the June 1912 marriage of her daughter, Ava's mother lived just under a year, dying in April 1913. The young couple continued in Woodstock for three more years, moving to Atlanta after her father's death in December 1916.

In Atlanta they lived on Drury Street, then a dead end, with their house next to the last one on the street. Ava and Warren had no children during the four years they lived in Woodstock with her parents. Their first child, Ava Frances, was born in their Drury Street home on 14 June 1917, five years after they were married.

On 26 January 1919 the young couple joined the Druid Hills Baptist Church, which had been founded on 1 July 1915. Dr. F. C. McConnell was the first pastor, to be succeeded by Dr. Louie D. Newton.

On a weekday in April 1918 a young couple, Parks Warnock and his wife, rented from Ava Sewell an apartment in
the Drury Street home. Warnock said the upstairs apartment, reached from the rear of the house by a separate entrance, was well furnished and "just what we wanted." When
Warren came home from the road on Saturday, he discovered that he had been selling work pants to Warnock's father, who was a partner in Wallace and Warnock General
Merchandise Company of Chamblee. Warren and Ava took
the couple to Druid Hills Baptist Church the next morning.

Warren was gone all week, but Warnock reported that
each weekend "as soon as he got in he'd check to see if we
needed anything." The Warnocks remained there for four
months, until July 1918, when he was called into the service.
In May 1919, his service completed, Warnock bought a house
on North Highland, and they joined the Druid Hills Baptist
Church, renewing their acquaintance with the Sewells, who
had moved to Sinclair Street.

The apartment-renting activity was characteristic of Ava.
One of her children remarked, "My mother was a frugal person, frugal to her dying day. Daddy was a more expansive,
generous person. My mother was the one who would see
after money." She did just that. Warren, who termed her "a
great lady," spoke often of her efficiency and her prudent
saving, which provided substantive assistance to them as a
couple and to him as a businessman. They made a good pair.
They had a fund of common sense and no social pretense at
all.

In the spring of 1921 while the family was living on Sinclair Street, their second child, Charlotte Elizabeth, was born
in Georgia Baptist Hospital on 21 May.

Firmly and prosperously established in Atlanta, the three
Sewell brothers, seasoned salesmen and jobbers, were soon
to add another dimension to their business—the manufacturing of clothing.

· CHAPTER II ·

Manufacturing

The willingness of the New York merchants in late 1921 to give the Sewells a chance to work out of their bind, coupled with the continuation of banking support in Atlanta, enabled the three brothers to work at turning things around. In three years of zealous endeavor they achieved a profitable jobbing business; and as they worked at it, they considered the future.

For years Warren and Robert had talked about making men's clothes themselves instead of purchasing them from manufacturers. In New York they had seen the shops where suits were made. They felt, and so did their brother Roy, that if New Yorkers could make men's clothes, surely Southern men and women could. It was their conviction that Southern workers, especially small-town and country people, could work and sew as well as the New York work forces. A belief in the capability of Southern workers sparked them, rather than any pointed view on the efficiency of machines or industrialization.

Around 1921 they decided to begin making men's clothing in Atlanta. For a shop they rented the upstairs of 99 Mitchell Street, near the federal building, and arranged for Cliff Hughes, Sr.—who worked for a pants factory in Roswell—to leave his job, join them, and supervise their manufacturing.

The upstairs factory had six and finally twelve machines in it, and for a cutting room there were two tables pushed together. The Sewells were now both manufacturers and jobbers. But when it became apparent that no profit was being secured on their manufactured clothing, they ceased making clothes. After two years they closed up the factory, and their manufacturing supervisor left, managing to get his old job back in Roswell. The Sewells continued their jobbing, securing their goods primarily from New York merchants.

Cliff Hughes, Sr. (left), and his brother, Howard, a machinist for Warren Sewell Clothing Company, in Howard's pool hall, Atlanta, 1920s. Both moved to west Georgia with Warren.

About a year later, in 1924, they again tried manufacturing men's clothing, having persuaded Hughes to resign a second time and come to Atlanta. And this time they stuck with it. "At first," said Hughes's son, "they made only pants, all my father knew. They wanted into the coat business. They rented an upstairs room across the street and hired a Knoxville fellow to make coats. But they wouldn't fit a closet door."

The Sewells tried two or three other fellows to supervise the making of coats, with equally poor results. Coats were not made in the South then, and it was only after they sent Hughes to New York for six months of experience that the Sewell plant could turn out an acceptable coat. The business prospered, grew larger, and Hughes bought into the company.

On 20 May 1927 Hoyt Broadwell, sixteen, joined the firm, hired as a floor-sweeper. He said the firm's top-level structure consisted of the Sewells, Cliff Hughes, Sr. as manufacturing supervisor, an outside salesman, Cecil Graybill, and A. R. Lovvorn as inside office man. Within a few months Broadwell took over as shipping clerk when the present clerk, only twenty-six, died suddenly.

When the plant became crowded, it was moved a block and a half south of the Mitchell Street location to 127 Forsyth Street SW, in a two-story building with the factory upstairs and stockroom below. It was to remain in operation at this location until January 1930. The plant was always small, with never more than twenty-five machines.

Eula Norton, whose husband "was the first man to press a pair of pants for Warren Sewell in Atlanta," began working for the Sewell brothers in 1928 at age twenty-two, inspecting pants. Later when the brothers began making coats, Eula worked buttonholes, sewed on buttons, put back pockets in pants, and at times inspected the finished product.

In 1928, she said, people wanted to work, needed work, and were glad of the $1 a day, five and a half work days, amounting to $5.50 a week.

A cousin of Warren has memories of his father taking him to Atlanta when he was a young boy and getting him outfit-

ted with a suit and an overcoat at the Sewell factory on Forsyth Street. Both items of clothing were economical in cost
and of heavy and long-lasting fabric.

A number of factors nudged the brothers toward moving their manufacturing operation out of Atlanta. Warren
cited the lack of economical housing; after testing Atlanta,
they found they could not manufacture profitably "because
there was no place for workers to live." Also, there were
parking problems, difficulties with downtown congestion,
and lack of economical space for a plant. Eula Norton said
Warren always "wanted to get out where he could construct
a building of his own." All in all the Sewells felt that a smaller
community would offer advantages to a manufacturer employing a large number of people, mostly women, for the
sewing needed to put together men's suits.

Long before they decided where they would move Warren had been accumulating information on possible sites. A
young man from Bremen once met Warren on the street in
Atlanta and they began to talk. When Warren learned he was
from Bremen, he drew him out about his home area, especially Bremen and nearby Tallapoosa, asking about the trains,
people, jobs, and farming.

Warren said that once the decision was made to leave
Atlanta, it was plain that Bremen was a real possibility for re-
location, for they were seeking a distribution center. Almost
all shipping was by rail, and as Warren said, "Bremen was
the only place they had a cross line railroad on the Southern
Railroad, which we had always considered the right way to
operate." The Central of Georgia, which ran from Savannah
via Griffin to Chattanooga, crossed the main line of the
Southern from Atlanta to Birmingham at Bremen. Also, the
Southeastern Express Company and the Railway Express
Company served Bremen.

The town of Bremen not only had two railroads and two
express companies available, but also boasted a healthy supply of labor, especially women workers, plus good schools
and several churches, no significant housing problems, and
no congestion. There was only one small plant there, a

Bremen's railway depot, 1920s.

*Southern Railway engine,
early 1900s.*

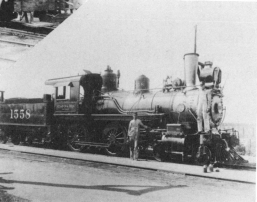

Central of Georgia's
Nancy Hanks, *1910.*

Mandeville Mill shirt factory, which in fact at that time made cloth not shirts.

Most important, the site was near home. The family home in Graham, where their parents, brothers, and sisters lived, was thirty-five miles from Bremen. A cousin of Warren said Warren moved to Bremen for three reasons: "It was uncrowded, there was good labor, and it was home."

There had been some talk of a location in Madison, Georgia, where there was a rail crossing, but there was really never much of a contest as to the new location. Warren had a strong sense for home, for the area and people of his youth. He was possessive about his home area and grateful to be possessed by it. Graham-Bremen-Bowdon had a sort of lasting enchantment for him.

In anticipation of a move to west Georgia and the inauguration of an expanded and different business, the three brothers took action in 1926 to modify the structure of the company and to clarify the public perception of the business's ownership. To replace Sewell-Longino Company, they in June 1926 renamed the firm Sewell Manufacturing Company and took in as an additional partner A. R. Lovvorn of west Georgia, who was to be in charge of the office and financial operations. Warren says that when the move came, they owed no one anything and "had what little money we had in cash."

In Bremen J. J. Mangham owned a private bank, and when news of a possible move reached him, he offered his services to Warren, hoping to induce him to locate in Bremen. He and Warren Sewell were already good friends. Exactly what transpired between them is not clear. There are stories that Mangham's bank loaned the brothers $100,000 to get underway in Bremen, but there is substantial doubt that at that time any west Georgia bank had $100,000.

As a location for a plant the Bremen city council gave the Sewell Manufacturing Company the city-owned light plant on a lot parallel to the Central of Georgia railway. In ninety days Warren constructed a small building heated by a boiler on the Bremen lot. In December 1928 Cliff Hughes, Sr. and

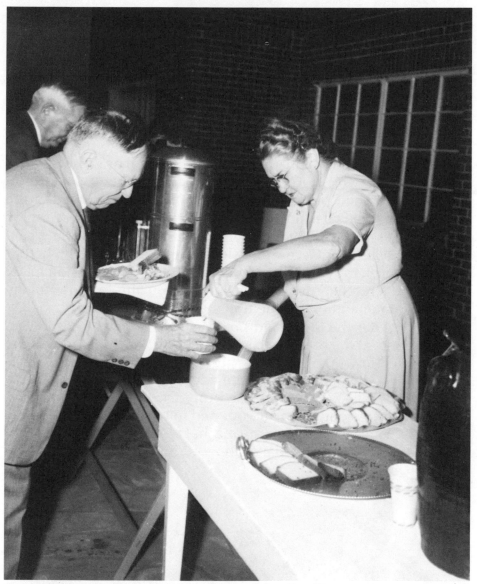

Banker J. J. Mangham and Ava Sewell.

several others moved from Atlanta to Bremen and commenced operations. A laborer said that his duties were to get the fire going in the boiler, sweep the floor, and tote water and ice in buckets to the sewing room. Another employee described the beginning days by saying, "Mr. Warren had everybody a-working all the time. Everybody did everything, anything you could put your hand on." Meanwhile, the Atlanta plant continued operations.

As Christmas of 1929 neared, there was a lot of work on hand that needed to get out—"a heaping pile," said one worker, "the lining of the armholes." And Warren Sewell said it must be done before there was any Christmas vacation. "We went to a-working and we finished. We knew Mr. Warren probably had promised to deliver and that he needed the money to pay us."

On 6 April 1929 the Bremen plant burned over a weekend, resulting in a complete loss. The question was whether to go back to Atlanta or rebuild, and the swift decision made was to erect a larger building in Bremen and to continue the Atlanta operation for the time being.

"After the fire," said Lois Waddell, a Sewell employee, "we met at the Bremen schoolhouse and signed up those who wanted to work in Atlanta." Her husband Lee Waddell was one who helped construct the new plant, using a mule and a scoop shell. Work progressed rapidly on the new building, which was completed and opened in two months, by 22 June 1929. The speedy action meant that none of the Bremen plant people returned to Atlanta to work in the plant there.

Farmers Bank,
Bremen, Georgia, 1920s.

Bill's Place,
Bremen, Georgia, 1920s.

When Plant Number One was finished, the Sewells for the first time had all operations together—cutting, garment making, pressing in the basement, and materials storage in the front end of the building.

After the newly constructed Bremen building opened things moved fast. The workers saw little of Warren; he was on the road selling all the time. Said one, "We knew Ridley Lovvorn bettern Mr. Warren because he wasn't there. He and the others were out on the road selling."

In general the sales force came from around Bremen—a school or farm boy became a stockroom employee and finally went on the road, usually with an older salesman. The key staff people for the new enterprise generally were from Bremen. The only outsider brought in was a designer to improve the fit of the clothing they produced. The workers who had jobs in Bremen on the day of the fire came back to their posts. Eventually all the Atlanta workers came to Bremen to work. This work force was expanded by hiring locally, one or two each week, until the total force was at forty. With the hiring of this work force, some of the latent reasons for Warren's move from Atlanta to his home area surfaced. One of his staff recollected that as the applicants for jobs lined up in the Bremen street "he stood, with folded arms, watching. He said, 'I told you the Graham people would come. If the print of the hoe handle is in their hand, hire 'em.' "

From his years of labor in the field he knew how the hoe felt in the hand, how red-dusty the fields were, how difficult it was turning the mule and plow at the end of the furrow. He felt he understood these people, how hard and how simple their lives were, how much they needed work, and he believed these country people would make splendid plant workers. He was convinced that people from Graham and Bowdon and Woodland had an idea about the dignity of honest labor, were willing to work, and should have been working. So he hired them, some in their teens, others who were 35-40-50, all needing work and willing.

In part Warren regarded his business as an assistance operation, of benefit to the people at large. In business for a

Sewell Manufacturing Company, Bremen, Georgia, July 1936.

profit, he was also there to provide steady employment, to enable people to better themselves, to paint and improve their country houses, even to buy a home and a little acreage.

From the start, said one of the original employees, "the plant was just like a big family of people. He hired people who wanted to work. He didn't have to build here but he did. All knew why Warren Sewell came—to help people who were hardly making a living. From the beginning Warren Sewell was just pure gold." Another said, "He never made any showing, you'd think he was just one of the farmers around here."

So began the deep respect—and in some ways affection—that developed between Warren and his workers. It would nourish and sustain both sides in future crises.

Some of the workers from Atlanta knew nothing of Bremen. When the Norton family moved from Atlanta to Bremen in September 1929, they found it was "just a dead little town," with muddy streets. They had a model T Ford and "we'd go to Atlanta every weekend. We couldn't stay in Bremen. It was too big of a ghost town for us." They would drive over the unpaved roads going back and forth to Atlanta. "We'd ride the train to Atlanta sometime when it would get so bad we couldn't drive."

Soon, however, they did not go back to Atlanta as often. Eula Norton said, "After we kinda got settled down and got us a house and everything, well, we kinda got weaned off from it. And now [1983, fifty-four years later] you couldn't run us out of Bremen." From her hiring in Atlanta at age twenty-two, she remained with Warren Sewell for forty-two years, until she was sixty-four.

The Bremen business was a success from the start. When cotton went up to eighteen cents, sales grew better. "You could buy a Warren Sewell suit for $3.50 to $6.75," said one worker, who described his job as "pressing coats, hauling them across the tracks for buttonhole work, hauling them back for pressing." When he braced Warren Sewell about moving both functions to the same side of the railway, his

Clerical Department, Sewell Manufacturing Company, July 1936.

boss replied: "You make just as much for toting as for pressing, don't you?"

In 1931 the Sewells scraped together everything they had or could borrow, and Warren made an extremely large purchase of blue serge material, at a time when the price was very low, fifty cents a yard. They began to make and sell a blue serge suit with a Warren Sewell label—"a 16-ounce blue serge so heavy it didn't wrinkle," said a stockroom employee. In the stockroom just across the railroad tracks from Plant Number One, these suits did not hang on racks but were instead put on tables and covered with sheets.

A retail store owner says he bought blue serge suits from Warren Sewell for $7.50 and sold them for $10. "That gave the merchant $2.50, which was 25 percent, and I was glad to get it. I sold a lot of them." So did many other merchants. The story in the industry and among salesmen is that the profit Warren Sewell made from selling this blue serge suit during depression years earned the firm its first million and provided the foundation for its future expanded business. Warren Sewell made suits out of this stock of cloth for years, continuing to turn a profit for the firm and for numerous retailers.

The sales forces worked on selling the chains as well as individual merchants and hit on the idea of offering these larger purchasers a private label in the suits—an approach that improved sales greatly.

In 1932 in the middle of the depression, Warren decided to build an additional plant in Bowdon, closer to his Graham home, which was just over the Alabama border. There were bread lines everywhere, and the unemployed were hungry for work. Construction of the Bowdon building gave jobs to workers in a hard-hit area—brick masons and carpenters at twenty-five cents an hour, common laborers at fifteen cents an hour, and drivers with mules to haul brick at three dollars a day.

Bowdon was a small town, with little opportunity for employment there. Further, Bowdon College, which was founded in 1847 and had educated scores of west Georgians

Cutting and Trimming Department, Sewell Manufacturing Company, July 1936.

(including all three Sewell brothers), vanished in 1933, merged into the new West Georgia College in Carrollton. The wounded and concerned Bowdon residents viewed the new Sewell plant as an affirmation of faith in the town, and they were proud of the new business.

The Sewell plant, which cost less than $10,000, opened in 1933 in grim economic times, paying workers 50 cents a day, $3.50 a week. This was steady work and an improvement on the bread line.

Roy Davis, who was transferred from Bremen to the new Bowdon location, said Warren raised him from $11 a week to $15, pointing out that the increase covered his house rent in Bowdon.

A Bowdon resident whose husband worked on constructing the new building went early the first morning job applications were taken for work in the new plant. To her concern, she found there was already a long line there. But in two weeks she received a postcard to report for work, having been chosen as one of ten new employees. Her schooling and some slim practical experience in sewing started her on a decades-long career in the Sewell sewing room.

Here as in Bremen Warren Sewell saw to it that the newly hired workers were country people. Many were from nearby Alabama, where he was raised. Said an old-time maintenance department employee: "He was very hard about hiring people. He wanted you to work. He liked people off the farm." Another said, "He picked people from families he knew, figured he didn't have to check on their background or anything." One who was hired and remained with the firm until he retired, Roy Lee McClung, said, "I just graduated from high school and went right to work. I had only hoed and planted cotton."

Many people from below Graham who were without jobs went to Warren Sewell's mother in Graham, asking help from her about jobs. She'd say, "Now Warren, you try so and so in the plant." And he'd say, "Yes, Momma. Yes, Momma," and would do it. "He had," said one plant employee, "a gift for the working people. He believed in people."

One story has it that when the Bowdon plant opened, a number of applicants were or said they were Sewell kinfolk, some distant cousins several times removed. Warren Sewell's reaction was to hire them all; they'll make it or not once they are on the job.

The firm had an acute problem in the distribution of its manufactured products. Its sales force was small. They could make suits, they could sell them, but how to get them out there? Robert Sewell was a top-notch salesman and a hard-driving, high-pressure, imaginative individual. As a partial answer to the distribution problem, he conceived of a group of company stores, all stocking Sewell clothing. Roy Sewell explained how the company stores operated, pointing out that this was during the depression, when one could rent a small store on, say, Peachtree Street in Atlanta for $200 a month on a thirty-day notice. Robert would find a hungry young fellow who had $200 and did not mind hard work, get him to open up, and Sewell Manufacturing Company would

Robert Sewell.

fill his racks with suits. When the manager closed the doors on Saturday evening, he sent a check for the suits he had sold that week. The rest still belonged to Sewell Manufacturing Company. "Times were tough. We sold the suits cheap, some as low as one dollar."

By 1932 there were forty such company stores, all over the country—up in New York, in Oklahoma, out west. The benefits of the Bremen location at a major rail crossing were apparent, for goods were shipped out rapidly to these stores by railway or sometimes by Southeastern Express or American Express.

Raymond Otwell, who joined Sewell Manufacturing Company in 1932, said that in that year he kept forty different checking accounts and forty sets of books. The managers made their deposits, while he kept their books and paid their bills. An occasional company store was operated by a Sewell relative. In Atlanta at Porter and Marietta streets the brothers' uncles Shelley and Paul Sewell ran such a store.

The company stores became a profitable part of their overall business. When times got better and Sewell Manu-

Buchanan Street, Bremen, Georgia, 1939.

Matchbook advertisement for the Red Oak Hat factory.

facturing Company began to make substantial sales to merchants and to develop an expanding sales force, they offered each store manager the opportunity of buying the store, or the company closed it.

The manager who wished to purchase his store gave Sewell Manufacturing Company a note, and when there was enough money in the checking account, the store was his. Once a manager who had been in business awhile called Otwell to ask if he had $8,000 to spare in his account, as he wanted to buy a house. He had more than that, having paid off his note long before. The manager saw no reason to take over the books and pay somebody to keep them, as the firm did it gratis. This manager died worth close to a million dollars, "all out of that little old store."

Robert Sewell, who created the company stores, was a superb salesman, "the dynamic, pusher-pressure type," as one observer described him. Robert decided in the early 1930s to leave the family business and go it on his own. He pulled out of the partnership, selling to Warren, and went into the hat business in Red Oak, Georgia.

Later when Robert became ill, Warren bought Robert's new hat business, to get the struggling firm's problems off his brother's mind. Sometime later, when Robert's health improved, he wanted to buy the hat plant, and Warren sold it back to him. Making hats was a troublesome business; on the whole, it did poorly and was of grave and deep concern to Robert. Both Warren and Roy missed him greatly in their business. Ill and despondent, Robert took his own life in the fall of 1939.

During World War II when industries began to convert from peacetime to wartime business, the Army Quartermaster Department asked Sewell Manufacturing Company to produce Eisenhower jackets and army pants. Warren secured 200,000 yards of cloth and shifted to making uniforms. The plants continued military production all through the war, until 15 September 1945. The cash profits were handsome.

Sometime in 1945 Warren began to think about how the family and the Sewell Manufacturing Company had been affected by the war and what the final, overall impact would be. He gave this matter prolonged consideration. He was fifty-seven, his brother Roy forty-seven. Warren owned about fifty-five percent of the company stock, and several employees owned shares also. Altogether the stockholders had a healthy and sizable group of older children, most of them away in the war but heading home in the near future.

Warren himself had two sons-in-law that would soon return from the service and a sixteen-year-old son. Roy had two sons. Cecil Graybill, a vice-president, had three sons in the

*War Bond Sale, in front of H. J. Reaves Store,
Bowdon, Georgia, World War II.*

Sewell Manufacturing Company letterhead, showing clothing label and plants.

service, while A. R. Lovvorn, vice-president and treasurer, had a son in the Navy. Silvey Landers, a salesman, had a daughter. All the stockholders were aware of and concerned about the problem of the children; how to prepare for the future and find room for them all?

Warren said he could get along with his brother in operating the firm but wondered if the cousins and in-laws could get along with each other. He frequently commented that in a family business the first generation makes it, the second generation takes it, the third breaks it. Moreover, he occasionally added that it generally takes just three generations to get from shirtsleeves back to shirtsleeves.

In addition to the question of these sturdy and numerous offspring, there were some disagreements in the early summer of 1945 among the principal stockholders in the Sewell Manufacturing Company. These disputes were amicable but there was some degree of emotion present. Warren Sewell owned more than fifty percent of the stock, was the founder, and had been and was the leading spirit in the business. In the operation of the Sewell Manufacturing Company, he spent little effort on negotiation or consultation with the others. He had been the leader in the firm and simply continued to be. He dealt with a heavy and decisive hand with the rest. The others chafed somewhat under his method of operation and, as one close observer said, "From what Mr. Warren told me and what I heard others infer, the other stockholders got together and agreed let's sell out to Warren."

Meanwhile, Warren, detecting discord developing among the coalition of relatives and comrades, had concluded that some change in the business would be necessary. He discussed with his family the possibility of changes and their implications, talking with his wife and his son Warren and making visits to confer with his two sons-in-law.

Roy recounted that open discussion of a split in the Sewell Manufacturing Company came when he went to south Georgia to see his brother Warren, who was working cattle on his farm there. Warren put him in the largest guest bedroom and gave him a fine country meal, after which Roy told Warren he wanted to split their partnership. Warren's re-

Warren and Roy Sewell seated together among Sewell Manufacturing Company staff.

sponse was, "Well, all right, brother. Let's do it in good spirit. After all, we nursed at the same breast."

They quickly began to assess the value of the Sewell Manufacturing Company, to take steps to ease the capital-gains burden that would come with a sale, and to draw up an even-handed buy-or-sell agreement, on which Warren, the majority stockholder, would make a choice. Either Warren would buy out the other stockholders' interest in the Sewell Manufacturing Company and own it all, or he would sell his portion of the company and receive cash for it. Drawing up the buy-or-sell agreement did not take long. In ten days or two weeks when they met again on the matter, to the surprise of all concerned, Warren, who was perhaps in a better position to buy, elected to sell the Sewell Manufacturing Company to his brother Roy for cash.

Roy raised the $1.7 million for the purchase of Warren's share in the company, gave Warren a check, and the split was a reality, effective 15 September 1945. It took Roy some scratching to get together the purchase price. After he paid it he said he had $17,045 remaining, "close to nothing, but [I] was ready to operate, owed no one, believed I could do it—that I could outsell Warren."

There was never any doubt that Warren, divested of his interest in Sewell Manufacturing Company, would take the cash and go into a new business for himself. As soon as the essential decision was made between himself and Roy, Warren went down to the plant boiler room with Raymond Otwell and told him, "I'm going to sell and go into the clothing business for myself."

Roy described the arrangement in simple terms as giving Warren the nucleus to start a new business, that is, the Bowdon plant and its own office and stockroom in Bremen, right on the distribution railway line. The Bowdon plant that Warren secured was not operating, having remained dormant and its work force unemployed since the military contract work had ceased months ago. There was no pants factory in the Bowdon shop, and the one in Bremen went to Roy; Warren had to provide his own.

Roy had an operating plant and access to the labor force in the Bremen area, just as Warren's plant-to-be in Bowdon had workers available nearby for its future operation.

The buyer, Roy, had the right to keep any Sewell Manufacturing Company employees he wanted except for a few people—three or four—who elected to move across the railroad tracks in Bremen with Warren's new outfit. No employees, including salesmen, were to be hired by Warren without the agreement of Roy.

One salesman with Roy, who felt squeezed out of getting any good territory by the sons of various owner-families, asked for release so he could sell with Warren. He was refused until he began to nose around for a building to open a hat factory. Roy said, "If you feel that strongly, I'll release you."

The split and move across the tracks was done amicably and with grace. There were occasional difficulties, some more humorous than substantive. One of Warren's workers in Bowdon missed a water cooler, which he was convinced the buying group had removed. Then somebody made off with his mattock and shovel. This was too much, and he protested: "Mr. Warren, the way you said this thing was put together was give and take. And Sewells come in here and took. They got everything including my shovel and mattock." Warren's response was, "Aw, you go uptown and get yourself another one and forget it."

A newspaperman who put out a company publication for Roy said there was never a criticism or comment in their sales meetings about the competing firm, Warren Sewell Clothing Company. And said Will Roop of the split, "They were great family people, never any malice. There were no arguments, never a cross word."

The brothers separated their businesses completely into two generally competing firms. There were no agreements on lines of clothing, territory, prices, selling areas, nor was there any continued assistance or cross-servicing. Said one who accompanied Warren into the new firm: "They wrote us a check. We put it in the bank and started again. The brothers gave no special help to each other, but remained just as interested in each other as brothers could be."

The split would establish in one small town, just across the railroad tracks from each other, the headquarters of two competing firms, both aggressively making and selling clothing—Roy's Sewell Manufacturing Company and Warren's new firm, the Warren Sewell Clothing Company.

Why did Warren Sewell sell? There are many explanations. Concerning the split and his decisions, Warren Sewell is generally given credit, especially by those who returned from the service, for viewing things with a far-reaching eye. After all, he had created the firm, lived with it, developed it, and thought out the best thing to do. He felt, and others shared this concern, that there were too many young men in the official family who would head home, seeking employment; there was not room in the company for all.

However, he sensed perhaps more clearly than others that there was room and opportunity out there in the market for another enterprise. As one veteran Sewell salesman, who knew him well, explained, "The Sewells loved economic opportunity just like you and me. They could see the coming expansion in the clothing industry, and I think they felt you can operate two businesses as easily as you can one. When I go into one of these little towns and sell a fellow, he wants this line exclusive. I can't sell the fellow across the street, but you in another firm can. Two Sewell companies expanded the market."

An equally compelling point to Warren was an understanding of himself and of the past, present, and future of a family-owned, family-operated business. His driver, Clyde Newell, who had keen insights on Warren Sewell, put in simply: "He wanted to be Mr. Sewell."

On the day the decision was made to sell Warren went to his Graham farm, where he found Eugene Hughes, a friend and employee, cleaning out a spring. As they sat by the spring Warren told him of the decision. Hughes recounts that he asked his employer why at his age—"I thought of him as already old"—he would risk going into a new business. Why not make a position for himself in the present business, or move into the hat business, or retire? Warren Sewell replied that he was going into the clothing business for himself and that he would rather leave his children a business and work opportunity than a million dollars.

Gene Hughes.

His driver was right: Warren Sewell wanted to be the senior person; he had an ingrained distaste for the inhibitions of working in a conglomerate. He did not want part of something, for that made him second. At the same time he was generous in his assistance to others, always ready to give them a chance to do their own projects, in their own fashion, and in a business that was or would be theirs.

One Sewell-watcher said of some of the business ventures he aided: "He didn't mind helping you get started, he didn't mind letting you go, but he wasn't going to share it with you. He wanted not only to give you a chance, but he wanted to be doggone sure that he still had his chance, to be himself, to be not second, to be Mr. Warren Sewell." He knew the business, he knew the family—in particular his brother Roy—and he knew himself. He sensed there simply was not room enough for all in a single business.

He was fifty-seven years old when he sold his business, and the cash he received was substantial. He could have quit. But he had not forgotten the vision that led him from between the plow handles. Now in the very area in which he had plowed the tough and unrewarding land he was operating a successful business, giving dignified employment to the farming people he loved. He could not leave these people and their problems. This work of his was life, it was pleasure, it was meaningful. Being in business was another way of continuing a useful life, a way of not being second.

Once Warren sold he had no cloth, no machines, no trained labor, no customers. Altogether these factors represented a pot of troubles, which was just what he wanted. He could not live without challenge. Warren had the agreement of both his sons-in-law to go in business with him upon their release from the service. One, Jack Worley, an Air Force pilot, would go to Monroe, Louisiana, as a partner in Buccaneer Slacks, a firm in which Warren and Ernest Marchman of Bremen, a former Warren Sewell Clothing salesman, were equal partners. The second, Lamar Plunkett, an Army officer on duty at West Point, would come to Bowdon to be general manager of the Warren Sewell Clothing Company plant to be established there.

One of the first new arrivals at Bowdon in 1945, Cole Bell, reported the circumstances as follows: "Wasn't nobody down here but me and him and Mrs. Feilds, his secretary, and Mr. Plunkett. Just a few of us, didn't have but five or six hands working here." The Bowdon staff was increased slowly. In addition to Lamar Plunkett as general manager and Roy Davis as plant supervisor, there was as designer Virgil Strickland who had been in the business a long time. Others were to be added.

Plant workers, though untrained, were there in west Georgia to be hired. Warren Sewell's greatest problem was not people but cloth and machines. In the division of assets he had secured some machines, those in the pants shop and in the coat shop in Bowdon. These machines were not particularly proficient and were indeed ragtag. It was not that they had been palmed off on him, but there had been no renovation or replacements for years. Machinery for manufac-

Warren Sewell Clothing Company plant, Bowdon, Georgia, about 1947.

turing clothing had not been made for several years; sewing machines were scarce.

In addition to possessing little machinery Warren had no cloth, lining, or trimming. The wartime mechanisms were still in place—not only for pricing but also for allocation of materials, supplies, and machinery.

In sum the situation was quite confused. Warren Sewell sold his business on 15 September 1945. Before that time the priorities of the War Production Board had been released, allocating piece goods, machinery. Yet the allocations were rescinded, then reestablished in a matter of a week or two. Warren had authorization for not one sewing machine or one yard of cloth. To secure a priority or an allocation one needed in all cases a formal approval, and generally a business history was required to secure approval.

Warren Sewell had a history, but it was in the other firm, Sewell Manufacturing Company. When he sold it he sold his history, and along with it his right to needed machinery and cloth. He had no license to buy. Even when someone said he had plenty of cloth, he could not sell unless Warren possessed a license to buy—something he in indignation called "a ticket."

The search for these tickets proved tough. Raymond Otwell made a trip to Washington in search of them, with no success. Warren and Lamar Plunkett went to see Georgia Governor Ellis Arnall, asking that he intercede in their behalf. He dictated a strong wire to Washington authorities that said, "We have soldiers walking our streets wearing ODs long since tailored and long since washed and cleaned, and they need civilian clothes. And here we have a man expert in the clothing business and ready to provide jobs and the needed clothing, and I ask that you give him the go-ahead." Governor Arnall followed up on the matter, pleading the case for work and clothing.

Lamar Plunkett was a friend of Senator Walter George from south Georgia, and almost every morning he telephoned the senator's office in Washington, asking for help in getting credentials to buy. Senator George knew Warren Sewell, but he had some difficulty understanding the ramifications of how he made himself ineligible to purchase cloth and machinery. Plunkett talked to the senator's son, Herb, who explained to his father and advised him what to do. Finally a telegram came from Washington, saying they had approval to buy both fabric and machinery.

With the priorities and allocations in hand—those elusive tickets—Warren Sewell went out in the marketplace after what was needed to make clothing.

As to fabric there was little to be had. Clothing people took anything they could obtain. His former concern, Sewell Manufacturing Company, had a good standing in the marketplace in getting a proportionate share of cloth. Warren went to various people he had formerly bought from and told them he was going into business for himself and had the necessary authorization to buy. "I don't want one yard of cloth that belongs to Sewell Manufacturing Company. Now what are you going to give Mr. Warren Sewell?"

Some people came forward and helped him, and those people he never forgot. One who helped with cloth was Hutchinson of Peerless Woolen Mills (later Burlington) Mills. In later years when Peerless needed business, they could call up Warren Sewell and he would send a couple of trucks up and load them with Peerless fabrics.

George Moses was a former Warren Sewell salesman, operating his own business and grateful for past assistance. In New York on business for his pajama factory, he made the rounds to all the cloth suppliers he knew, telling them of Warren Sewell and his need for cloth: "He wants no goods of others, only free goods, no under-the-table payments. Looks like a hick and talks like a hick, but isn't. Will be a great manufacturer." Gradually Warren built up a stock of cloth.

He searched for and bought some machinery himself, traveling often to Richmond, Virginia, and once to Philadelphia to buy from a Greek. Warren ruefully related that when the Philadelphia deal was agreed upon and the seller embraced him, kissing him on both cheeks, he knew he had been cheated.

To secure most of the machinery he turned Gene Hughes and Cole Bell loose to buy. "I don't mind your spending my money," he told them, "but know what you're doing with it." No machinery was to be purchased on the black market. Hughes and Bell claimed they knew little about machinery but they learned fast.

In Dalton, Georgia, a factory making parachutes for the army had just closed. They bought a truckload of machinery there, following that with a second truckload out of Alabama. In Goodlettesville, Tennessee, they found a whole factory that made pants, owned by Breezy Wind of Knoxville. They bought it, disassembled it, and moved it to Bowdon. In this lot Bell said he purchased what he thought was a swatch-binding machine, though it proved to be a useless hat-binding machine. "I paid $18.75 for it, and I never heard the last of it." A year later, said Bell, you could buy new equipment, "and by then we had people who knew what they were doing." Not one piece was bought on the black market.

In this way Warren Sewell secured what he needed to get back into the clothing business—the scraped-up machinery and what he termed "a little remnant of cloth." To these he added newly hired west Georgia workers. Young people were streaming out of the services and returning home. The area had its share, and Warren Sewell Clothing Company hired numbers of them.

The Bowdon plant had lain dormant with its work force idle since September 1945, when the making of Eisenhower jackets ceased. The first people were called back to work on 17 November. The factory and pressing room were served by an old sawmill boiler, which they fired up. It built up steam, and they began to make clothing.

On 7 December 1945, less than three months after selling out, Warren Sewell's new firm sent out to merchants his first shipment, sport coats. "After a while," explained Lamar Plunkett, "we began to get fabric and to get churned up and start a business." As material became available the new firm settled down into more normal and sustained production.

By February 1946, five months after formation of the new firm, Warren Sewell had remodeled a warehouse near the initial plant building in Bowdon, built a cafe close to the two shops, and constructed a large warehouse on the grounds. Both the old and new buildings were well lighted by natural and fluorescent light, were steam heated, and had been made into comfortable working quarters.

The new building, of imitation brick, was 50 by 150 feet, and was for manufacturing pants. It was white throughout, with hardwood floors and gleaming shellacked tables for cutting. The pants shop employed fourteen people on opening day, with more being added each week.

The old building for manufacturing coats and vests had been rearranged and repaired; more room was made available through removal of the cafe. The office was moved from the front to the side of the building and enlarged.

With shipping and office facilities in Bremen and a remodeled plant in Bowdon, the new firm, Warren Sewell Clothing Company, was poised for growth.

*Warren Sewell Clothing Company's
first sport coat, 7 December 1945.*

Lamar Plunkett, who had joined the firm in November 1945 after leaving Army duty at West Point, was superintendent of the Bowdon plant. He and his wife, the former Frances Sewell, and their small sons, Richard and Tom, would soon move from Atlanta to Bowdon.

Roy Davis was assistant superintendent and in charge of maintenance. Employed as a machinist in Bremen in 1929, he had transferred to Bowdon in 1933.

Joe Catoggio of Brooklyn, New York, was head tailor, in charge of quality control. He had worked in New York for Rogers Peet and as a tailor for Saks Fifth Avenue.

Mrs. Lee Waddell was in charge of the coat shop. She was originally employed at Bremen in July 1928, a short time after the firm moved from Atlanta. She was named supervisor of Plant Number Two in Bremen in 1932 and was transferred to Bowdon in 1940.

J. E. Gardner headed the pants shop, having been with Warren Sewell when he opened in Atlanta in 1926. He made the move to Bremen, working as a cutter. In 1931 he was made superintendent of Plant Number Two in Bremen, then transferred to Bowdon.

V. W. Strickland, who headed the cutting department, had been with the company eighteen years, working first in Atlanta, then Bremen. In 1930 he was sent to New York to study designing and grading patterns.

Supervisors in the pants shop included Alma Davis, Pauline Jackson, Ralph Fowler, Leonard Brock, L. J. Norred, Alvin Batchelor, Mrs. W. G. Kent, and Mrs. Lovie Sanders.

The office force of the Warren Sewell Clothing Company in 1945 consisted of Alva Davis and Emily Carmichael, and the salesmen were: Silvey Landers, Eugene Hughes, Hoyt Broadwell, Marvin Worley, E. E. Greene, Joe Fry, T. A. Fry, Ted Copeland, Nels Arnston, J. W. Fristoe, A. J. Larger, Earnest Marchman, and Warren Sewell himself. Lois Whitehead managed the plant cafe.

Alma Batchelor was supervisor of the vest shop, with Lee Waddell, Julian Feild, and Annie Norton supervising various steps in the manufacturing process, while James Davis oversaw production control.

For administrative support Warren Sewell leaned on Raymond Otwell, financial manager; H. G. Darnell, his chief accountant; J. H. Pritchett, credit manager; Leland Strickland, shipping; Parks Warnock, Jr., order control.

Earlier in Bowdon there had been limited production, with no more than 120 employees. The size of the work force there increased rapidly to about 1,000, recruited from the surrounding farms and small towns. Many of them would remain with the firm for years, such as Ed Morris. Just back from the service, he was hired at Bowdon, remained there a couple of years, then moved to Bremen and eventually became head of the shipping department.

Business was good and got better. Thirteen million young people were out of the service, and most wanted clothing. A stockroom employee at the time said that in 1946 they would have 600, 700, 800 suits come into the stockroom, and there would be merchants standing there, begging "give me something I can sell, give me six, give me three." "I remember one time," said another worker, "that we couldn't make enough suits. They come here and bought suits before we could even press them. They'd want one or two or three and would take them unpressed."

Warren Sewell's new firm kept going and growing, as did involvement of his family in the business. By the early 1950s his son and two sons-in-law were working for Warren Sewell Clothing Company. His son Warren had done summer work in the business at Bremen and Bowdon and on the road in Oklahoma and Kansas. He came to the business full-time in June 1950, upon graduation from the University of Georgia.

Warren Sewell's son-in-law, Jack Worley, had returned to Bremen from working in Louisiana and was on the road, selling as his father had done before him. The other son-in-law, Lamar Plunkett, continued as manager of the Bowdon operation.

After ten years as manager in Bowdon Plunkett decided to go in business for himself. Using the stock they owned in

Warren Sewell Clothing Company and cash they raised, he and his wife Frances formed LaMar Manufacturing Company on 24 October 1955. Warren Sewell and his wife Ava said they wanted a part of the new company, and each bought one share at $50.

The new firm was strictly a manufacturing concern. It did not have a selling organization and did not have capital to carry accounts receivable. It made goods for Warren Sewell Clothing Company and would also manufacture a world of items for a West Coast firm, Rothchild-Kaufman.

When the employment office for the Plunketts' new Bowdon firm opened, there were prospective workers standing in line for three blocks, waiting to be interviewed. "I mean," said Plunkett, "the finest people you can imagine and anxious to work." John Cook, a worker personally recruited years before by Warren Sewell and at the time running the pants shop for Warren Sewell Clothing, came to be plant manager of the new firm.

Lamar and Frances Plunkett.

Four years later in 1959 Warren Sewell brought an old friend of his to see Plunkett—Sam Goodman, who had been in business for years but was losing his line of goods. He was well known, could sell anywhere, and wanted a line of goods. With Warren Sewell's blessing, Plunkett in 1960 set up another firm, a distributing company called Bowdon Manufacturing Company. The older LaMar Manufacturing Company now made clothing and sold to Warren Sewell Clothing Company, to the West Coast Rothchild-Kaufman firm, and also to the newly created distributing firm in Bowdon. Sam Goodman now had a line of goods and went on the road.

It was not long before Warren Sewell brought in another friend, Billy Green of Dallas, Texas. Retired from selling sporting goods, he had a showroom in the mart in Dallas and a lease on it for a good while. He wanted to show the Bowdon line, so another salesman and a new outlet were added. Later other salesmen joined the Bowdon Manufacturing Company, including Plunkett's son Thomas when he graduated from Mercer University.

The resulting organizational relationship has been retained, with both Warren Sewell Clothing Company and Bowdon Manufacturing Company buying clothing from Bremen-Bowdon Investment Company and from LaMar Manufacturing Company, and each distributing through their sales staffs.

The history of the Warren Sewell Clothing Company has remained relatively simple. In 1926 the three Sewell brothers in Atlanta, knowing that they were moving the firm's location, modified the structure and name of their business. Having bought out George Longino's interest in the jobbing firm Longino-Sewell, they changed the name of the firm to Sewell Manufacturing Company.

Nineteen years later in 1945 Warren Sewell sold his majority interest in this firm to his brother Roy, who continued to operate it as Sewell Manufacturing Company.

When Warren Sewell sold his interest in the family firm, he then founded a new organization, the Warren Sewell

Clothing Company, which he owned outright. He subsequently began to operate and develop this new firm. He continued to do so for twenty-eight years, until his death in 1973, when Warren Sewell Clothing Company was one of the ten-largest manufacturers of men's clothing in the country, with plants in Bremen and Bowdon, Georgia.

Since the death of the founder in 1973 the president of Warren Sewell Clothing Company has been his son Warren. He also served as acting chairman of the company from July 1973 to September 1975, when he was succeeded by Jack Worley, from September 1975 to December 1983, and Lamar R. Plunkett since January 1984.

For Bremen-Bowdon Investment Company Warren Sewell, Jr. served as acting president during July 1973 to September 1975, when Lamar R. Plunkett became president and Warren Sewell, Jr., chairman.

The influence and activity of Warren Sewell and his firm served to encourage formation of a number of other firms in west Georgia, some by family members, others by friends and business acquaintances.

Board of Directors, Warren Sewell Clothing Company, 1984
(Left to right, seated): Jack Worley, Lamar Plunkett, Warren Sewell, Jr., Valee Sewell. (Standing): John Cook, J. Mac Smith, Richard Plunkett, Thomas Plunkett, Robin Worley, Mark S. Swindle. Not present: Raymond Otwell.

·CHAPTER III·

The Diligent Boss

A fellow bank director said of Warren Sewell that one of his strong points was that when he thought he was right, he was pretty sure he was right. His workers and associates had the same perception. A worker explained, "Mr. Warren, now I respected him and loved him, but he was the boss and he wanted to be the boss. He was strong and what he ran, he ran. Mr. Warren was uneasy in anything where he couldn't say how it was to be going. He wanted to be on top of the thing."

A veteran Sewell sewing-room employee did not find this characteristic dismaying, for with simple straightforwardness, she said: "He was the easiest man to get along with, if you'd just sit and listen to him talk. And then if you'd do what he wanted you to do, you'd get along with him."

On the other hand when a Sewell worker did not do what was wished, he was apt to hear from the boss. Thinking back

over forty-three years of work with Warren Sewell, another
worker commented: "He didn't mind letting you know when
he spoke that he was Mr. Sewell. Yes, sir, called me in many
a time and told me so and so, like once when I worked on
Sunday." However, he added that at the same time Warren
Sewell was deeply interested in his people, not just his im-
mediate staff but all of them, and he did his best to treat them
fairly and pay them well.

The characteristic of wishing to be boss, springing from
those early farm days in Graham, had led Warren Sewell out
of the family business and would influence and temper his
participation in venture capital efforts and joint business en-
terprises.

A Bremen observer described Warren Sewell as "one of
that rare breed, the Christian businessman. He believed in
doing business up-front and straight-out and no under-the-
table anything, and treating people fairly, and just practicing
what Christianity is all about. And he didn't do that just on
Sunday."

A Bremen businessman talked about Warren Sewell's
business personality as follows:

> Temper, yes I'd say he had it. If you crossed him you paid for it,
> one way or other. He was a reasonable man. It took a lot to get
> his dander up, but once you did it was very difficult to smooth
> it. He knew what he wanted and he knew how to get it, which
> is the mark of a successful man. He was fair. I don't think he ever
> took advantage of his position. He was generous. He paid peo-
> ple for performance. He penalized them when they didn't per-
> form. He put a great stock in loyalty. He'd rather have a loyal
> fellow that wasn't quite as successful, not quite as competent,
> than a disloyal one that had all the ability in the world.

His criteria for hiring his staff were not known. Most records, if there were any, were in his head and not shared. He
surrounded himself with men who had no higher education
but who possessed great loyalty and dedication. He en-
deared himself to them, encouraged them to study and learn.
And they stayed with him and kept his confidence, respond-

ing to his interest with a devotion that was genuine and rare indeed. Nobody on the staff would have done anything to hurt him.

As for hiring his staff and selecting his professional associates, he was strong on personal knowledge and on bloodlines—a good man had good sons. He felt this approach beat any kind of personal background sheet.

Over the years he had observed a young Bremen resident, Tom Murphy, who as a boy occasionally came with other Bremen youngsters to ask Warren Sewell for a contribution to their baseball team. When Warren Sewell saw Tom Murphy, a Democrat and a promising lawyer, growing in ability and stature, he pondered the matter and finally telephoned Murphy to say he would like to come to see him.

Murphy insisted that he walk across the tracks to call on Warren Sewell, which he did, curious to see what "the Old Gentleman," as he respectfully termed him, wanted. Once his visitor was seated, Warren Sewell said he did not wish to fly under any false colors, that he wanted to retain Murphy as counsel and asked what it would cost. Tom Murphy told him, but inquired as to what Warren Sewell had in mind for him to do. What sort of cases would he handle; how would he represent him?

The Old Gentleman responded that he really did not want him trying a lot of cases, "Tom, I just want you not to be agin' me." Murphy walked out of that meeting as retained counsel for Warren Sewell Clothing Company and handled a few matters for the company over the years. Murphy considered the relationship a fine one: he was never asked to do a political favor, and Republican Warren Sewell never once gave him a campaign contribution.

Warren Sewell was not especially high on college training. He told James Pollard, a native of the area, when he hired him away from the telephone company in the Carolinas, "I'm going to hire you in spite of the fact that you have college training." Will Roop, a wholesale grocer and contemporary of Warren Sewell, said, "He had a knack of picking young people and pushing them ahead. I don't think he ever made

Father-Son Teams, Warren Sewell Clothing Company, about 1953.
(Left to right) Warren Sewell and son Warren, Marvin Worley and son Jack,
Ted Copeland and son Ted, Virgil Strickland and son Archie, T. I. Landers and son Silvey.

a mistake. If he did, I never heard of it. Lots of his people turned out simply great." With his personal staff as with his workers, he believed in training his own. For example, he encouraged G. E. Wasdin to go to law school and to accounting school.

People bonded themselves to Warren Sewell for a long time in happy, productive work. One plant department head said, "I could have made a lot more money other places. But like I told my wife, Mr. Sewell has been good to me, and I am not willing to leave him." He added that any assistance he asked for he got—a new piece of equipment, a raise to keep a valued employee from going elsewhere. "Mr. Warren didn't think about these being little things, and he was always ready to help me out."

As far as business matters were concerned, Warren Sewell depended primarily on Guy Darnell, Sr., G. E. Wasdin, and Raymond Otwell. He listened to everyone, but he paid special attention to these three men.

He had a reasonably simple way of measuring the worth of an intended business action. If it was legal, he did it. He did not have to worry about the outcome; he had a dedicated and enthusiastic staff. As one Sewell worker commented: "He had people around him who helped him. I can't imagine that Mr. Warren lost much sleep at night thinking about his help."

This is not to say that his staff did not worry. One said that when he began work he did not know if he could do what Warren Sewell wanted, and he worried. Warren Sewell had him write his worries down in a notebook and look at the list after six months, saying he would find "it either didn't happen at all or it happened like you thought it would."

One of his staff pointed out that it was not prudent to tell Warren Sewell he was wrong. "You'd better suggest that he might consider so and so; not 'no' and not 'must.' Just suggest. He would take a chance to show you that you were not necessarily right."

His counsel said that as far as business ethics went Warren Sewell was very straightforward, never lied to him,

Gelon Wasdin.   Guy Darnell.   Raymond Otwell.

never lied to any business contact, "but he could make a deal, buy a piece of land, sell a suit, settle a claim."

In dealing with his staff he asked for their opinions, waited, then did what he wanted. A friend he depended on in conferences and for assistance in family and estate matters said: "He wanted my unvarnished opinion. I wasn't to be a yes man. Fifty percent of the time he didn't take my advice. He heard it out and waited and decided his way."

A great many people believed Warren Sewell had the ability of foresight or certainly the knack to see more of people's future than they themselves knew was there. He gave them tasks to do and furnished no details. He placed a great strain on his people, but he believed they had the capacity and he believed things would get done. He was an excellent judge of character who was disappointed only a few times.

Some say he had vision or forecasting ability in business matters also, "long-reading foresight," as one said. Warren Sewell put in a coal-firing boiler when the plant began. In 1983 the firm replaced it with a much larger one, having decided to stick with coal for the future.

Still, there is ample evidence and testimony that Warren Sewell's actions were not always predicated on astute business judgments. Luck and attentive hard work had much to do with his success. "It was good," said one staff member, "that he had devoted staff to look after him."

The same man who made a spectacularly fortunate and profitable purchase of blue serge cloth could install in his plant an inadequate and expensive cooling system based on sprayed, air-cooled water instead of air conditioning. He had listened to the salesman's claim that with air conditioning, "you've got the doors locked, the windows locked, you got no fresh air, you're breathing the same air over and over again."

His amazement at the suggestion that the Georgia Baptist Hospital in Atlanta should look into the use of computers was, according to another hospital board member, genuine and sufficiently strongly put to table the matter for the time being.

Warren Sewell was strong on assistance to those who worked closely with him. "He wanted to know about your problems," said Ed Morris, "and he wanted to help you out. You'd better not tell him your problems if you didn't want his advice, because he was going to tell you exactly what to do." His second wife Ina said that people frequently telephoned him for advice, "and if I heard him say once I heard him say a million times, 'Now let me tell you exactly what to do.'"

He was both business-wise and educated in the ways of his fellow men. He had wisdom and common sense. He made judicious decisions and enjoyed assisting others to make them. He helped with the most difficult decision and with the simplest. It might be the question of a new business in Bowdon or the concern of a sharecropper on his farm who had enough money to either buy a new pair of working boots or get married.

His personal support for his staff was thoughtful and substantial. A young married man raising a family and hoping to borrow for a house was told to go to the bank for a loan. "Tell them if they turn you down they are to call me, I'll help. And if that isn't enough I have some stock in a little bank in Canton where you can get the money." It was no surprise that the local bank generally helped. The same staff man commented: "You could depend on Mr. Sewell's help. He didn't butter you up with a lot of fancy words. When he told you something you could hang your hat on it."

For new staff members he bought life insurance with their wives as beneficiaries. Said one, "It was a different relationship. He was very good to us. We felt that we were part of his family. I never failed to make more money next year than I did the year before, whether the company did well or not. He was interested in all his people, not just his close staff. He did his best to treat them fairly and paid them well."

Warren Sewell had a little fishing pond near his house in Bowdon, and he would let staff members go there to fish. One staff member said that every year when he headed off for his week's vacation Warren Sewell always checked to see if he had enough money to cover his expenses.

What was Warren Sewell really like at this time in his life? He was a man of contradictions and in this hardly unique. From his father he inherited a well-proportioned body and was also full of vigor, had a keen wit, and demonstrated a genial talkativeness, a love of humor and jokes. From his strong mother he inherited a calm and unhurried nature, almost-perfect self-control, a kindly compassion, a ready generosity, and incredible perseverance.

With little formal education himself he deprecated extended education for most, while sending young men and women to college or professional training because they had promise. He made almost a fetish of health and physical well-being, yet followed a routine that would have killed off many.

In his personal life he was notably wholesome. He had a remarkably good mind and was loyal, sympathetic, and brave.

Warren Sewell,
"Big, tall, well-proportioned, with a ready smile."

As far as his neighbors and workers were concerned, his little foibles and eccentricities were ignored, though surely in private they chuckled at them. After all they were no greater than the peculiarities found in most people. As they saw him he was the sort of honest, thoughtful, independent man they admired among themselves. True, his work was different, but it was honest labor and he paid unceasing attention to it.

Warren Sewell's appearance and voice set him apart from others. One of his Bowdon College classmates recounted how in the early 1900s it bothered her that his trousers, undoubtedly homemade, never met the top of his shoes. But when asked about his physical appearance, she said with spirited candor, "There was nothing wrong with Warren Sewell's looks." And indeed there was not. The wife of a company employee recalled how as a bride of twenty-three she first met Warren Sewell in her Bremen home. "I thought him the tallest man I ever saw, with the heaviest eyebrows. He overshadowed me, yet he was warm and friendly. We loved him from then on. He was more than an employer."

A women plant employee found him "big, tall, well-proportioned, with a ready smile, a neat but not fashionable dresser. Warren Sewell didn't overdo his dressing."

An Atlanta banker recalled him as a young man, both as to overall appearance and dress: "He was a right good-sized man, an imposing rugged sort of fellow with black hair and dark eyes, as plain as an old shoe, no fancy dressing, a very straightforward individual." The banker went on to say that Warren Sewell fit in well in Atlanta. He was not long on conversation, "but you could look at him and tell he was a man of strength and substance. That alone made people take note of him and see him in a favorable light."

A vigorous and robust man of sturdy stature, he had a strong and expressive face, a thoughtful one, with a full brow, firm chin, and dark eyes. When he spoke with anyone, he looked directly at him. All in all if his appearance was not strikingly handsome it was strong, intelligent, even distinguished. His alert manner, erect bearing, and quick stride afforded a general impression of controlled energy.

Warren Sewell, 1963,
"An imposing rugged sort of a fellow with black hair and dark eyes,
as plain as an old shoe."

One of his retail store customers reported that he always wore a dark blue or black suit, baggy, and one or two sizes too big but comfortable. The pencils, pens, and papers he carried were more than he had pockets for.

His shoes were size twelve or thirteen bi-sized kid, black, and made of very soft leather, with a hard cap on the toe, easy and comfortable. He wore white socks, parted his hair in the middle, and wore a hat most of the time, occasionally even in his office.

He always dressed conservatively, said one worker, "though not like he was going to a funeral or a wedding." He was seldom seen without a coat and tie. Once in a while, when with the church deacons at an outdoor meal in the pastor's backyard or on a fishing trip, he would omit the coat and necktie.

His necktie seldom matched the shirt or suit in color or style. This tendency, plus his frequent questions to associates about the color of a piece of cloth, led many to consider him color-blind.

He would move from office to farm or farm to office with his usual conservative dark suit, pockets bulging, tie mismatched and awry, shoes dusty and unshined. But his workers and associates did not see him in this way; they saw a man who was rugged, responsible, capable, and plainly dressed.

When he took his pleasure working on the farm, he dressed like a farmer and sloshed through the cow lot in rubber boots with his workers. Occasionally, when he returned from farm to office, his appearance showed it. His brother Roy, who was a fastidious dresser, was always bothered by Warren's lack of concern for his attire. He said he once gave Warren a dollar to go get his shoes cleaned and shined. "He took the dollar and went on to work without doing anything. When it came to his personal attire he didn't care much about it. I've seen him wear shoes re-soled two or three times and cracked all across here. But he was a nice looking man."

Sometimes visitors were surprised at their initial sight of him. A salesman bringing a Jewish merchant to the plant for the first time pointed out Warren Sewell sitting in his open-air office, talking on the telephone—in his baggy suit, with the tie around on the side of his collar. The visitor said, "That can't be Warren Sewell." The salesman acknowledged that most people expected a fashionably dressed, well-turned-out fellow, adding, "Mr. Sewell don't worry about wearing them clothes, he just makes them."

He did not splurge in dressing. He wore the suit he made, wore it casually and without undue attention to it or concern for style. He did not dress like a clothing salesman and appeared to be just an ordinary person. His staff had to connive to get him to have new suits made for himself, using the fiction of photographs that had to be taken for some coming event.

"Clothing didn't mean anything to him but something to sell," summarized a mill representative. To him a suit of clothes, the product he made, was something to be sold and shipped out to other people to wear and enjoy. In this process he found pleasure and a sense of accomplishment, but he never derived joy out of putting on the suit and wearing it. The pleasure, the sense of satisfaction, was in the making and selling, not in the wearing. The suit—its production and marketing and the consummate pleasure of having struck a mutually beneficial bargain—was of great importance to him, but never in the sense of personal adornment. He put his emphasis on matters he considered weighty, and personal dress was not one of these.

While his appearance and dress were ordinary, his voice was not. "He had a loud voice," said a cousin, "you could hear him from here to the nearest crossroads." For many years his office was merely an unenclosed, bannistered-off place, open to sight and hearing. He talked on the telephone so loudly that every worker in the building knew all of every conversation. His personal counsel lived in Carrollton, miles away, and said, "Mr. Warren had a voice. He didn't need a microphone. He just raised the window in Bremen, called my name and said hello, and I'd say yessir in Carrollton." When he sang in church at full volume, sometimes his family moved over a little.

About Warren Sewell's powers of memory, there is what one generally hears—and then there is the rest of it. One fellow worker said, "He had a mind that retained a great deal. He didn't bother much about keeping written records." A salesman said, "He could keep it all together. He had a mind that could keep all facts in his head. Day to day, month to month he had it all in his head." A relative said, "He had a remarkable memory, he never forget anything."

Soon after the kitchen in the Atlanta Springdale Road home was redone, his wife Ava discovered that he had written numerous telephone numbers on the newly painted wall, as high as he could reach, and he knew exactly where every one was located.

A staff member described how one would see him in his automobile, making notes "and driving, more or less. He'd come to Bowdon from Bremen and he'd have his inside pocket just stuffed with little notes, and he'd work from there." It might be an accumulation of a month, with merely two or three words pertaining to an item, but he knew what was there and could work all day out of that pocket. Occasionally when he left his office to visit in the plant, his secretary would telephone to his destination, asking those there to be sure to have him search his pockets "because there is a lot of information in there that needs to be taken care of."

When asked how he kept up with everything, his second wife Ina said, "He made lists." The manager of one of his plants said his boss was always making notes, that he believed Warren Sewell, the early riser, deciphered and studied them when he first got up.

A distinction can be made between his use of notes and his lack of dependence on records. He had a lot in his inside pocket and a lot in his memory. He kept notes on whatever was at hand—on church bulletins, on blank checks, on tissue paper. But frequently he made no personal notation of occurrences, especially of loans or gifts made out of his pocket. He always carried a big roll of bills and a supply of counter checks. If people who spoke to him needed money, he gave it then and there. His friend Will Roop was a banker, and if

Warren Sewell needed a counter check and did not have one he would say, "You got any of Mr. Will's stationery around here?"

Many times he considered that the atmosphere and circumstances of a request for financial help negated any need for recording. Being too formal or having to wait spoiled the event. He made his mind up quickly and that was it. His lawyer worried and protested, for this kind of approach generally prevented any tax benefit. Warren Sewell listened some, but not much. Now and then he would make out a counter check payable to the person asking for a loan, have him endorse the check, and Warren Sewell would then cash it from his roll of bills. This procedure gave him a record of the transaction, but no one knew what he did with the endorsed checks.

Will Roop (left) and Warren Sewell (right), about 1978.

Warren Sewell knew his workers by first name, and he greeted them so. Of all the things he did, this one meant the most to them. Not only would the plant owner talk to and listen to members of his work force, many of whom could not ordinarily secure the attention of people of authority or position, but he really knew them; he addressed them, as one said, "by my very own name."

As great as his retentive power was, it sometimes failed him, and his standby address, used to persons known and unknown, was "Hello, Good Friend."

Not only did Warren Sewell possess a striking appearance, a voice that mattered, and a renowned memory, but he also had a democratic and unpretentious nature.

When a young World War II veteran from south Georgia was discharged and came for his terminal leave to Bowdon, his wife's home, he was impressed by Warren Sewell's easy, democratic nature. He had never seen the owner of a large clothing plant sitting down in a public, small-town restaurant, eating breakfast with his janitor. The young man remained in Bowdon and went to work, though not for Warren Sewell. Over the years he continued to find the unpretentious nature of Warren Sewell to be genuine, and all his life he was impressed by it.

One of Warren Sewell's women workers commented that "he was so down to earth that it was amazing. I could relate to him. He could talk to me as well as he could other people in the community." He was one of the neighborhood, born and educated there. He liked the same things they did, belonged to the same social and fraternal groups.

Both an Atlanta banker and the cloth salesmen who came to see him found him to be as plain as an old shoe. The salesmen for large knitting mills never had to make an appointment to see him. They might wait right in the office with him while he talked on the phone, but he saw them all, and promptly.

His wife Ina said walking on the street with him was an experience, sometimes a slow one. "He always had time to stop and talk to anyone. In fact," she added, "he stopped and spoke to everybody, young and old, black and white."

Plant employees had no reluctance to leave their work stations and come up to him in the plant with their problems. And when he wished to speak to them, he took an easy and familiar approach. A woman supervisor related that on election day he stopped in her work area and inquired if she had let her workers off to go to the polls. She had, but two were not registered, and he quietly urged them to register so they could vote in the next election. "I want the good people, like you, to be represented," he said.

"Temper?" said his second wife Ina. "I don't know. I never saw any. He was a controlled individual but a positive man." In a similar vein his friend from boyhood onward, Will Roop, said, "Yes, he did have a temper, but he controlled it mighty well." It was readily apparent when he was mad or upset. A plant associate said that when he got really stirred up, and his upper lip got thin and white, "Then," he advised emphatically, "go, go—go far away."

The storm passed reasonably quickly. He could be harsh but not vindictive, although he would remember the incident for a long time. A cloth salesman told of his firm getting at outs with Warren Sewell over an order for linen cloth. In this event Sewell felt he had not been treated right. The salesman was a couple of years getting back into his good graces and remarked, "I'd rather suffer another man's wrath than Warren Sewell's disappointment."

In 1930 Warren Sewell issued a large eye-catching calendar in bold black print with red numerals. In one country store where the calendar was displayed a wit took his pencil, circled the firm name and noted, "The Factory Without Wheels." Somehow word got back to Warren Sewell and months later, when the fellow came to see him about a selling job, Warren Sewell let him know that the "Factory Without Wheels" had no place for him.

It took a lot to get his dander up, and once done it was difficult to smooth it. He seldom raised his voice to command attention or to interrupt conversation. But he could get his

Sewell Manufacturing Company Calendar.

point across. One morning he dispatched one of the shipping clerks to Bowdon to pick up clothing and truck it to North Carolina in a hurry. When he saw the clerk at 4:30 that afternoon, still trying to get everything together for departure, Warren Sewell was clearly exasperated. However, he merely looked at the worker in disgust and quietly said, "You're still here? I could have sent any dumb body on this trip." He once told his wife, "I pray for patience every day." When his supply ran out, he could use his temper to good effect.

He had a deep singlemindedness about him. "If he got it in his mind," said one of his supervisors, "you couldn't change it." He trusted his own judgment and own capacity to set a course, make a decision. Commented a country banker: "He had a quick mind. He could concentrate on a single idea and proceed to see it through."

He also trusted his own view of people who worked for him. With an easy directness that sometimes puzzled his associates, he gave them heavy responsibilities and challenges, knowing that they did not feel completely qualified. He had learned a great lesson in leaving the plow and the farm behind and striking out on his own.

There had to have been times when he felt inadequate, but he had not turned away. And now he put others in the same position, believing they could do as well, even if they felt incapable at first. He directly pursued this course over his lifetime and was seldom disappointed in the people he challenged.

His singlemindedness surfaced in the priorities he assigned himself. His wife Ina laughingly said that he put God first, the business second, and his family third. Without question he loved and cared for his children and all his widespread family and tried to show it by providing for and assisting them. But because he pushed so hard getting his business established, he did not give some of the family matters much time. As a man building a business he left to his wife primary responsibility for rearing the children and caring for them. His son Warren commented that business was never off his father's mind.

On Sundays as soon as he was home from church, he went immediately to the telephone and spent the afternoon talking to salesmen in various states, checking, encouraging. "Mr. Warren wasn't much to talk about anything except business," said one of his employees. "His mind was most on the Warren Sewell Clothing Company, on his business. He enjoyed talking to you when you talked about the company."

Warren Sewell's personal conviction of the correctness of what he was doing made him a formidable business operator. He could suspend decision, mull over an idea or a problem for a long time until he was perfectly sure, then quickly speak to the point. Such precision in speech and decision was the outer indication of his inner orderliness.

When he was buying in New York or at the mills and was pressed by the circumstances, he would say the matter would have to wait, as he needed to consult with his associates. One of his staff snorted, "He never consulted his associates."

Because of the certainty of his mind, it was difficult to predict his behavior. His driver said, "You couldn't figure him out. When you're thinking one thing, he's thinking of two." Sam Hubbard remarked that just about anybody he knew he could second-guess some, but not Warren Sewell. "You never knew what he was thinking until he was out with it."

Combined with his certainty about his actions was the fact that he was a man in a hurry. His father was termed "a minute man" by one of his neighbors, who said Willis was always in a hurry, as was Warren's grandfather Levi. Warren inherited the family trait. These three Sewells were each first-born sons, and history is filled with accounts of how such children, challenged by their circumstances, developed into men aware of the value of time and singleminded as to its use.

As a young drummer Warren faced a prospective employer for a job one afternoon, was curtly turned down, and the following morning before seven was headed to catch the train and return to his old employment. Stopped and hired, he turned in a new direction without pause.

Ina, his second wife, echoed what many said: "You know, the Sewells were always too busy to do anything much with each other. They were in too big a hurry." She had a family of her own, a big family, when they married. This was at a period in his life when he had time or was willing to take time to appreciate and enjoy family life in detail, with his new family and his old one. It was something he had not done fully before. While this gesture was late in coming, it was sweet and real to them all.

Warren Sewell liked the word "frugality," said his pastor Louie Newton. "He said waste is murder." And he carried this feeling into his life and his work, for one of his staff commented: "He got the best out of everything he ever bought and everyone he ever hired."

He came by this frugality naturally. His mother scrimped and saved for the family, and she instilled a sense of economy in her eldest son. As a drummer he traveled frequent-

ly with a Douglasville, Georgia, cutlery salesman named
Huffine. When they arrived on the train at a town, they would
not hire a rig to haul their sample cases to the hotel, where a
bed for the night cost three dollars. Instead, Huffine and
Sewell would carry their luggage to a boarding house three
blocks away, where for a dollar they could spend the night
and get two meals.

His secretary Mrs. Feild said he "was canny and
thoughtful with money, never careless. However, he wanted
his salesmen to travel first class, to make a good impression,
not to stay in dinky hotels. The very first time I made a plane
reservation for him I made it in the economy section. He said
he was a big man and needed room. Never again."

He was hard to shake from his customary and frugal
path. Once on his way to Hawaii he arrived at a customer's
house in California carrying a wicker suitcase with a rope
around it. "May I ask why you don't buy a suitcase?" his

Willie Sewell, Warren's mother.
She instilled a sense of economy in her eldest son.

hostess asked. "I don't like buying things for myself. Oh, everybody gives me suitcases, but I have my own."

He was a diabetic and his hostess found him boiling a needle before reusing it. She told him "not in this day and age," bought him disposable syringes, and to her surprise he used them on his travels and found them worthwhile.

While not personally extravagant or interested in luxuries for his own use, he accommodated himself gracefully to his wife's deep interest in antiques and assisted her in wide and considerable purchases.

His inherited and personally developed sense of economic but not parsimonious living carried forward to his children. "I mean," said a neighbor of the Sewells, "that family don't operate like they got money." His daughters, Frances and Charlotte, and his son Warren continue his tradition with their saying, "Show me the bargains."

Warren Sewell carried his sense of frugality into his manufacturing business. A retail store owner noted that Warren Sewell "was a frugal man who believed in getting his money's worth and in giving the usual money's worth." He was constantly observant of labor-saving and cost-saving possibilities in the clothing plant, such as installing a machine that in one operation would do all the pressing, including the sleeves. "He was real sharp on his operations," said the pressing-room foreman, "He wanted me to save everything I could in the pressing room all the way through."

One of his workers said, "Mr. Warren was not a tight fellow, he was a saving type of fellow." He added, "He was easy to get along with but he wanted you to take care of what he had. If he saw you break a coat hanger it would bother him. He did not want you to tear up what you were working with."

The lore of the stockroom about his sense of economy is almost boundless. A story from one worker goes that Warren Sewell came walking through the stockroom "and saw a little ole pencil about that long in the trash can. He picked it up and looked at me and said, 'You knooow, the dollars take care of themselves, it's these nickels I've got to watch. You could have been writing with that pencil all day.' "

Ava Sewell and her daughters—Frances on left, Charlotte on right, about 1953.

The stockroom floor was so bumpy you could stump your toe, and in answer to a worker's comment that it should be remodeled, he said you could manufacture clothing in a barn.

Cole Bell related that Warren Sewell frequently sent him to the Atlanta airport with suits for air-express shipment. Now and then his boss would ride with him to the airport, where he would get the streetcar for his Atlanta home. Bell drove an old farm truck that was pretty worn out. "You looked down through the floorboards and could see the pavement, and right about Villa Rica or along there Mr. Warren would begin to doze and sleep on me. One day over beyond Douglasville I looked at Mr. Warren, and he was a-dozing along. So I suddenly said, 'Mr. Warren, don't you think we need a little better truck to go back and forth to Atlanta?' He opened his eyes and looked down through the floorboards and said, 'Aw, Cole, we're making good time, just keep driving, this truck is good enough, we don't need another one.' And he never did buy another."

J. Wasdin said the only reason Warren Sewell put up with two fairly new automobiles for his own use was that someone else nudged him into it. "He didn't care for them or take care of them. They meant nothing to him." He did, however, find them worthwhile, telling one of his associates, "get you a Buick, they don't wear out till 400,000 miles."

He encouraged thrift and saving in his workers, lecturing them on living within their means. In each Christmas talk he included admonitions to his workers to save and prepare for the day when they wouldn't have anything. However, once a worker responded, "Save? Mr. Warren, I have to, on what you pay me." One employee said the plant owner was a great man on saving, that Warren Sewell got after him so much "I thought I had to save on account of him. That's how come I'm where I am today."

He set an example for his farm neighbors by never buying a piece of new equipment; he bought used and made repairs himself. A farm worker in Graham protested to him once, saying he should use finished lumber on the mule barn, which he had instructed be made of poles cut in the woods. Warren Sewell's response was that he'd stick with the poles: "There won't be anybody in there but mules, and they won't know the difference."

He urged economy on all. Once as he drove by a cross-roads store in Graham, he saw a sack of grain that had been tossed into the nearby hog pen. He stopped in the road and yelled at his neighbor, "What are you doing letting that two-dollar hog ruin that five-dollar sack of corn?" The wife of the neighbor commented: "He'd get us all right about being extravagant even if we didn't have two dollars to rub together. He could sure fuss at us about being extravagant."

Warren Sewell's concentration on economy led him to be careful of his time. The son of his longtime banker friend, J. J. Mangham, said that "he never wasted a minute. He was kinda like my father who had 500 acres in peaches, right at where Sewell's warehouse is as you come into town on 78. He looked after that peach orchard hisself until he was 75 or more. Lived to be 94. He and Mr. Warren was alike."

Warren Sewell had a healthy appetite, a Sewell trait, and ate well and heartily of plain but attractive country foods. His son reported that his father spoke of being hungry for certain foods as he was growing up, "but I ate the food on the table." He added that he had vowed he would never be hungry again. Good country food, simple but abundant and fresh, remained important to him all his life.

He saw that the Graham farm produced country food in abundance—vegetables, corn meal, sugar, ribbon cane syrup, beef, pork, chickens, eggs, peanuts, pecans, apples, scuppernongs—and that much of it was canned and also kept in cold storage in farm reefers.

A visitor to the Graham farm once found Warren outside under the trees with his black workers, happily cooking a big iron pot of beans and canning them. When the visitor commented on the resulting big supply, the reply was that one ought never run out of important things in life, such as beans.

At his Bowdon home he had a small fish pond and a large vegetable garden to which he devoted much attention each summer. He assisted in the canning and preserving on the Graham farm and at home. When his wife invited lady employees from the plant to their home to look over her antiques and share tea and homemade cookies, he showed up and proudly presented each guest with a jar of Sewell preserves.

One of his plant supervisors who occasionally helped him on the Graham farm lived on his own farm nearby. Every now and then Warren Sewell would come down there for dinner "and we'd feed him on just what we had, country ham and chicken and vegetables and fresh cake. He was one of the heartiest eaters you ever saw."

Among the foods mentioned as favorites of his were fresh corn, melons, turnip greens, corn pone, onions; the list goes on and omits little of the customary farm produce. When grinding sugar cane at his mill, he would drink the fresh juice, saying he could not get enough. He liked pecans and peanuts, sometimes carrying them in his pockets to munch on. Every year in August his pastor entertained the deacons of the church in his backyard for supper, and Warren Sewell took delight in selecting and bringing the best and juiciest of his watermelons.

When his diabetes forced him to modify his eating habits, he would sometimes take one of the stockroom clerks to lunch at Bremen's nearby M and W Cafe, treating him to a steak and apple pie with two scoops of ice cream, while he had a big bowl of lettuce. The clerk added: "He told me he wanted me to be strong enough to do the work."

He was easy to entertain, said one country housewife, "as he just was raised up on the farm" and loved the food they customarily had. Tea cakes and fried pies were particular favorites of his, and she said he could eat a gallon bucket full of fried pies. A staff wife who listened to him talk about chitterlings once got up courage enough to prepare them for him, and he gently told her she had "boiled all the good out of them." When she served watermelon as dessert at an outdoor supper, he moved from the table over under the arbor with his big slice, saying watermelon eating was not for the table.

The son of one of his staff members recollected that Warren Sewell came to his mother's house when he was eight or nine years old. He remembered it as a fancy dinner "where we had a table with goblets and too much silver." He had been lectured on food and table manners and was attempting casually to watch his sister for guidance, but was diverted by the sight of Warren Sewell expertly eating peas—and losing none of them.

A plant maintenance worker now and then went with him to the Graham farm, to help grind feed for the cows or work on farm motors. "Mr. Warren loved onions better than anyone you ever did see," he recounted, saying they stopped by the garden, where Warren Sewell and his brother Byrd happily pulled up spring onions by the handfuls. "He fed us dinner," the worker remembered, which included "real old time vegetables cooked in a black pot."

One of his daughters remembered that before he became ill and went on a restricted diet, he would thank the neighbor's wife who brought in a cake, then sit at the kitchen table and gladden the visitor's heart by eating it all.

His wife Ina summarized Sewell's view on alcohol: "He was very bitter towards whiskey. He was not a sensible man to talk to about it." He was staunchly and completely opposed to its use. He was drawn to this stand by not only his conservative-fundamentalist religious views but also by the experiences in his own family. Some were plagued by it, one died of it.

He advised his salesmen on the need for sobriety, underscoring that he did not need to employ men who would get drunk and throw their money away. "He just didn't believe in it," said one salesman. "You pretty well stayed straight or you didn't work."

He saw alcohol as an evil and was a teetotaler, though he did not press his personal stand on those who were not his employees. All his suppliers and customers were aware of the depth of his feelings and took polite care not to cause embarrassment.

There are unverified stories about how this lifelong non-drinker had a single beer once at a barbecue or did have a glass of wine at dinner aboard ship. But it remained for his two daughters to tell a charming story about their father and the strong punch.

In April 1959, following the death of his wife Ava the past November, one of the firm's best customers, Irvin Kaufman of California, invited him to his daughter's wedding. The Kaufmans were not only longtime customers but close friends; they had come to Georgia for Ava Sewell's funeral.

He accepted, asking his married daughters Frances and Charlotte to accompany him to the wedding by way of Hawaii. They enjoyed each other and the travel, which was a welcome contrast to the sadness of the dark winter just past. He paid for the trip, picked up the dinner tabs, and was the accommodating host. In Hawaii the daughters invited him to a hotel luau, and they appeared early to watch the process from the beginning.

He found the fruity punch the Hawaiian girls served to be delicious, unaware that it was laced with rum. He remarked, "This is the best punch I ever tasted in my life." And when the waitress came back he would say, "Little lady, I'll have some more." This went on through the removal of the pig, the hulas, the fire dancers, all of which he found enjoyable. "I believe this is the best party I've ever been to," he said, reluctantly acceding to his daughters' warning that the punch was full of sugar and not good for his diet.

He felt good, was vivacious and mildly talkative, happy with his daughters, away from home and from the recollection of sorrow and loss. His daughters, who never knew him to have drink elsewhere, found it a happy time.

Warren Sewell was big framed, husky, strong, and vigorous. He remained so long into life. "At 70," said Cliff Hughes, Jr., "he could walk you to death." He took a cold shower every morning and year-round he slept in an unheated bedroom with open windows. In his Atlanta home he added an unheated porch, which he used for his bedroom.

He slept well at night, putting his problems aside and taking them up the following morning. His staff worried and were frequently restless sleepers, but not him. All his life he could relax during the day by napping. Sometimes he would be talking, would quit in the middle of a sentence, go to sleep for ten minutes, and finish his sentence when he woke.

As a salesman he worked on the road in the worst weather, manifesting an attitude that ordinary health pre-cautions were not for him. On the road he traveled fast, mak-ing his calls and returning promptly. He would leave for his North Carolina sales territory on Tuesday's train, make his calls, and return Thursday, before people in the plant missed him. On longer sales trips when he grew tired he would stop for the night and have a glass of buttermilk, saying lactic acid was good for you.

He respected his physicians and followed their advice, but he fancied himself an amateur physician or at least a

Warren Sewell's Atlanta home, 1102 Springdale Road.

practicing prescriber. At home he supervised the administration of medicine to his children, leaning heavily on calomel, which they ruefully testified he sometimes explained would temper their naughtiness.

On his Dawson farm where thirty sharecropper families lived, one of his chosen duties was to visit the black workers who were ill, seeing that they had medicine or a doctor's attention. The reluctant worker who tried taking to a sickbed to escape fieldwork generally improved considerably at the sight of Warren Sewell and the thought of a second massive dose of medication, which consisted of his own version of spring tonic.

Aside from what he called blackwater fever, he was scarcely ill until well up in years. He believed in people being well, and he had a cure for every ailment. The problem was, however, that he prescribed the same thing whether it was what was needed or not. He carried his medicine kit on trips, including his fishing jaunts. One plant employee told how he became slightly ill when he and Sewell were returning by train from fishing in Pascagoula, Mississippi. The ever-present medicine kit was brought out instantly, and the employee sighed as he recalled, "One dose of that spring tonic, that's all you needed."

Once a stockroom worker who had a minor back ailment asked Sewell if he could use a high stool to sit on as he processed phone orders. The answer was no: "Next thing you know, boy, you'll have to have a cot to lie down on."

Warren Sewell had a keen sense of the humorous and the ridiculous. His second wife Ina, his daughters, his stepdaughters, his business acquaintances all testify to this trait. He believed in easy humorous talk, feeling it helped to dissolve mental and physical disparities.

A retail store owner said, "He liked to joke a lot, to tease." On one occasion he had secured advice from Warren Sewell about a prospective partnership in Rome, Georgia, and was warned to be careful about going in business up there, that the Coosa River at Rome was cold and deep. Once in a while Warren Sewell would inquire about the partnership,

Atlanta physician Olin Cofer and Warren Sewell.

asking if it went on well or was he dreaming at night that he was in the middle of the Coosa.

A customer from south Georgia sent Sewell a big sack of pecans for Christmas, and on arrival the stockroom crew checked it in and receipted it. The bag had a small hole in it, and everybody that passed by would get a pecan or two. A couple of days before Christmas he came out to get the pecans, found an empty bag, and learned that everybody in the stockroom had had a pecan or two off him. He yelled for his secretary and said, "Mrs. Feilds, file a claim." Then he added philosophically, "Just goes to show you, you can't leave nothing setting around."

Once Warren Sewell and two friends he had started in business, George Walls and George Moses, were driving from Bremen to Texas. One late afternoon they stopped at a farmer's stand and after some negotiation Warren bought a melon for twenty-five cents. Stopping that night in Monroe, Louisiana, Warren very carefully lugged the melon up the three flights of stairs to Walls's apartment and after supper cut it. It contained little meat and lots of seeds. Warren looked at it sadly and said, "I paid too much for the watermelon."

Once he sent a stockroom worker to pick up his Buick from the garage, then to go sell some cotton, pay the hands, and deposit at the bank. The fellow decided to play a joke on Sewell, and on returning from his trip told him there was something wrong with the car. "You know the buzzer on it if you're going sixty, well I had that thing on sixty and it started buzzing and I had to get your car up to ninety miles an hour before it would stop buzzing." "Boy," yelled Sewell, "that thing is there to tell you how fast you're going."

One suspects Warren Sewell's sense of the ridiculous extended to his own driving. An associate in the plant said that he frequently made notes when in his automobile, "while driving, more or less." An employee said flat out: "He was the worst driver in the world. The Good Lord had to be riding with him." Another commented that Sewell had learned to drive a buggy and never got over it.

Ina and Warren Sewell on board the Queen Elizabeth, *1961.*

On the farm Warren drove his Buick Roadmaster every-where. When he wanted to look at something down the field, he just drove there, road or not, he'd just go. It didn't bother him if the car got scratched or that there was mud all over the car, in the car, on the seats, on the floorboards. To his wife Ava's annoyance, the Buick was always muddy and worn looking.

He was unwilling for his grandson Tom, who was fif-teen and had a learner's permit, to drive on the farm, ex-plaining he was not old enough, while he barreled along in the Buick with one hand on the wheel, talking and paying lit-tle attention to hazards or where he was going.

A customer from the West, visiting Bremen, was taken for a drive by Warren Sewell. He said that as they moved down the road Warren would comment on the countryside, pointing over to the left at some scene, and the car would veer sharply to the left side of the road. Then the driver would spot something of interest on the right and again suddenly steer to the right, way over on the shoulder. After two or three miles of this they met another automobile, barely managing to negotiate safe passage, and Warren Sewell exclaimed: "Look at that fool. He ought not to be driving."

On one occasion when he was driving alone he drifted over the double center line and was stopped by the state patrol. He had no identification with him, and when pressed as to his occupation, he replied that it was "liquor running." They let him go. Once the state patrol in Alabama charged him with blocking traffic. He had no identification, no money, and no blank check. Someone from the plant had to be dispatched with $46 to set him free.

Another time he drove from Carrollton to Bremen, where the city was putting in a sewer line. There were signs everywhere: "road closed," "20 mph," "one lane," and so on. A stockroom worker recounted: "Well, lord a mercy, here comes Mr. Warren up the road to Bremen. He just plowed into a big pile of dirt, walked up to the stock room and asked us to get a wrecker down there. Mr. Warren said, 'It's a good thing I'm a good citizen, or I'd sue the city of Bremen, piling that dirt up right in the middle of the road, not a sign or nothing up.' "

He demonstrated the same aplomb when he returned from a European trip and was asked to the Methodist Men's Club to tell of his journey. He was careful to bring in casually that in Paris he attended the Folies Bergere, saying, "Those girls came out on the stage and they didn't have nothing on but those long white gloves."

When his wife was headed to the nursery to buy apple trees and scuppernong vines, he warned her to be sure and get both male and female ones. She asked how you tell, and he replied, "Turn 'em up and look at em."

A fine conversationalist, Warren Sewell enjoyed good, comradely talk. He was conservative and courtly in his language. His lifetime secretary testified that she never heard him swear, and his sewing room superintendents said they never heard him speak a bad word. He insisted that the Lord's name not be taken in vain in his presence. He followed the tradition of his father Willis, who was regarded for the cleanliness of his speech. Warren Sewell was from the farm and acquainted with the barn lots and the animals there and with rugged country talk and humor. His participation in such talk he limited to a select few friends and to private circumstances.

He liked to talk, to joke, to tease. A retail merchant, a customer for almost forty years, said that he could sit and listen to Warren Sewell talk all day long. "He could tell stories about the retail clothing business, the merchants he had bumped into, and interesting things that happened. He had a lot of sayings that he used. I'm sure he inherited them from his parents."

Whatever the source of his sayings, he had a lot of them, "quaint but appropriate," as one Bremen businessman said. "He was a man with a canny mind, not interested in common trends, but with his mind on another beat. He could turn his adages around to fit any circumstance." His sayings aimed at giving advice, directly or indirectly, or commenting on business matters. At other times, perhaps, they were merely folksy, homespun comments intended to reflect a country environment.

He urged his workers, "Make money when the sun's shining." And he suggested to them, "Put first things first. It will always work out," adding that it might not work out like you want it to or you think it should, "but it will probably work out best for you."

He early learned that he had to rely upon himself for decisions, for judging, and his favorite saying was: "Judge yourself and you judge the world." "Success," he said, "is 90% work and 10% brains."

As for business matters, his most commonly repeated saying had to do with individuality and the value of making purely personal decisions: "When everybody else is going to Rome, it's time for me to go to Graham."

The consummate salesman, the man who built a business on the need for selling, had an often-repeated adage: "Sell—and repent." He meant go ahead and sell and then be sorry when you find out you don't have it in stock, or go ahead and sell and then be sorry you sold it so cheaply.

For a staff associate who chided him on being overly careful, he said, "The big possum walks late at night."

He occasionally said, "A dollar will work for you as long as the world exists. But you are limited in how long you can work for yourself." In impressing his stepdaughters on how easy it was for money to slip away, he frequently said, "Money has no home."

As for comments of a more general nature, he looked at a politician who might not be all he seemed and observed with a country person's perception, "That fellow ain't no sweet-smelling gourd vine."

For the need to redo something he said, "We've got to lick that calf over again." And for a person who needed to be watchful he described the nervous and gingerly manner in which a horse crosses a wooden bridge, worrying about the noise and wondering if there is a hole in it: "You better watch out for the hole in the bridge."

When an unattractive dark swatch of cloth was offered to him for comment, he said, "It's morgue-y looking."

When he wished to emphasize his positive belief, he said, "As sure as gun is iron." And of one confused he commented, "He's like a lost hound in high weeds."

Warren Sewell was never like a lost hound about the clothing business. He had a concept of what it ought to be and how it would best operate.

•CHAPTER IV•

Clothes for the Common Man

Warren Sewell's concept of the clothing business started with the idea of making what Lamar Plunkett termed "the Ford or lesser model of clothing," where the suit, though essentially good, was very economical. The sales representative of a clothing mill said: "Warren Sewell was one of the best woolen buyers in the country. His suits didn't have hand-piped button holes or hand-sewn buttons but he'd give you the meat in the suit, he'd give you the material."

He sold suits at relatively low prices in an effort to bring a good product to a great number of people. "What it all boiled down to," said one retailer, "was that Warren Sewell made a suit that was just right. If it had been made any cheaper, they wouldn't have bought it; if it had been made to

Lamar Plunkett.

sell any higher it would have been too expensive for them. His suits were just right in price and in quality."

To make and sell such a suit, Warren Sewell felt he could not be cyclical in his plant operation. One of his prime convictions was that his plant was to keep operating. The clothing business is normally a cyclical one, with operations paced to sales, which results in ups and downs, openings and closings.

He knew that capital investment costs would continue in his operation, that indirect labor costs were ongoing. But his labor expense was not as great as in the North, for the whole range of wage scales was lower in west Georgia than in other parts of the country.

His vision of the responsibility of a businessman in the Bremen-Bowdon area simply did not encompass closing down and stopping workers' pay. He felt that for workers to earn a living wage, they needed continuity in work. And he needed continuity for retaining the expertise of his workers.

He had to instruct his farm people—give them total training—and with cyclical employment he knew many would be lost to him. As one staff person said, then he'd be "recruiting, rebuilding, retraining."

He might well not have had to rely on such an approach if his product sold for a higher price, but he did not have that kind of product and did not want it. He preferred to keep his plant open and running, keep his people working and on the payroll, and keep producing his type of clothing, which he knew he could sell.

In addition to his belief in maintaining an open plant, Warren Sewell held another premise about the clothing business—"you can't sell from an empty rack."

He was primarily and preeminently a salesman; selling was the spark plug of his business. He was sales-oriented from top to bottom. He did not want ever to miss a sale, and therefore leaned heavily on having goods on hand. One of his sons-in-law said: "He could move merchandise, and he was able to pick men who could also do it." A west Georgia banker commented that Warren Sewell's business always depended on sales. "In the depression when the Sewell brothers got started if you could sell, everything fell into place. If you could sell it, get rid of it, somebody could make it. This is the theory they have gone on all these years."

In brief Warren Sewell knew what type of clothing he wanted to make—sound but reasonable in price and manufactured in great numbers. He desired a large and constant inventory and an aggressive and capable sales effort. And, most important, he wanted a plant that operated year-round, allowing him to pay a good living wage to workers who would stick with him. The effects of these fundamental premises were profound on, first, his workers and his relations with them and, second, on his buying and selling operation.

One can sum up how he looked at the clothing business by saying he saw it as requiring three things—keeping open, keeping inventory and selling it, and keeping workers.

Warren Sewell was unusually successful in adhering to the premise of constant plant operation. In 1983 an old-line

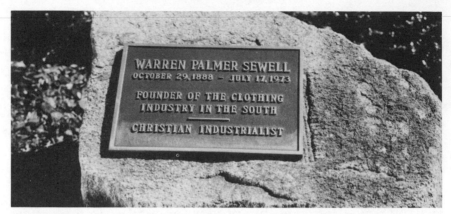

*Bremen, Georgia, monument to Warren Sewell,
"Founder of the Clothing Industry in the South, Christian Industrialist."*

worker said: "From 1945 to today if you worked for Warren Sewell Clothing Company you never missed a pay day." He went on to describe how in 1949 other clothing plants were closed, but not Warren Sewell, who was busy making clothing. "We didn't have the first order," he said, "and some folks thought we would not be working next week. We were thinking how long is Mr. Sewell's money going to last. Other plants were still closed. Well, all of a sudden the Korean War come on, and the economy began to pick back up. And we started staying there late; it was 10, 11 o'clock before I'd get home. We were packing and shipping clothes. And Mr. Warren said, 'See, boys, I told you all this thing wasn't going to last forever.'"

His workers were keenly aware of his determination to keep open; it affected them greatly. Asked if the plant ever closed for lack of orders or materials, a veteran of the sewing room replied: "Well, I tell you, I never was off but one time, and I wasn't off then enough to draw any unemployment. One time off was the only time during that 37 years I worked with Mr. Warren. I was safe, safe all those years I worked."

Essentially there were no shutdowns for lack of materials or orders. There were some times when the plant closed for minor periods—for example, to redo the machinery after signing a contract to make Army clothing.

Explained one worker, "The only times I can remember our being closed down was in between seasons they would do what they call clean up. Work the stuff out of the shop and clean the machinery, just the whole works. But it wasn't but a few days, not like a six-month layoff."

Once in a while the plant went on a 7-hour day and another time adopted a four-day work week. "But you're still working," explained one employee, "you can get by and you know you have a job."

One worker, who was asked why Warren Sewell operated in this fashion, said:

> One thing he was a good Christian man, that's one thing I lay a lot to. He tithed, and usually a fellow prospers by doing that. I remember the time back years ago that I knew he was taking out of his pocket to keep the thing going. We had stuff made up by the thousand garments. But he wanted everybody to make a living if they could, he was trying to help everybody he could. . . . They finally sold all that stuff and came right back. But I've always laid it to him being a good Christian man.

In 1937 the plant was virtually closed for three months while a new floor was installed. Said a worker: "They let us off, just worked one out of the family, you know, because business slacked off, and he didn't have much sales. We had to pick cotton for three months after they laid us off to buy us a little something to eat. Pretty tough. Finally Mr. Warren kept on until he had taken us all back." The worker explaining this one-time closing knew the hazards of seasonal employment, the value of constantly being on the payroll, and appreciated the philosophy of keeping the plant open.

Warren Sewell's view on keeping inventory was a product of his dirt-drummer days. He'd say, "You can't do business with an empty wagon." He always wanted goods. He wanted piece goods, and he wanted finished goods.

A plant manager explained, "He made clothes whether he had orders or not. To keep his plants working he would buy cloth, haul it in, cut it—all when it wasn't sold. He'd sell it finally, find someone, some fair price. Might not make any money, but he would do it, looking ahead always."

In 1932 Warren did a good bit of inventory building, to the puzzlement and concern of some of his staff. The pressing-room people came to Warren Sewell, saying they had even run out of hangers to hang up clothing as it came off the line. "Well, we ain't going to close this place down. Tell you what you do, you trot across that railroad track and see if we can borrow Mr. Peel Mangham's warehouse. I'm gonna show you boys how to fold these suits like we used to do before we had hangers."

They folded the suits and stacked them in the warehouse like cordwood, and then as more suits were made, stored them in other places. They were running out of places to store suits. But when the next slump came, the buyers for the higher-priced lines came down to Bremen and bought it all.

Ed Morris told of some of the problems accruing from the policy of keeping inventory.

> There was awhile there we had suits hanging in every building that was available. I had stockrooms all over the place, and it was scary. Now Mr. Sewell had a good customer, A. M. Bynum from Coffeeville, Kansas. He owned a store there and three in Tulsa, Oklahoma. He'd come in here twice a year and thank God for Mr. Bynum, cause he moved a lot of goods out of here. We'd sell him a lot of times three or four thousand suits at one time. He didn't pay as much for it as others did, but he had the money and he paid.

Bynum knew exactly what he was getting, had a big building to store it, and in that area he could sell it. When he came in the stockroom, Ed Morris would ask him what he did with all that stock he ordered before, and Bynum always said: "Sold it to my brother."

A plant worker gave this reaction to Warren Sewell's policy: "He'd make talks to us in the plant and tell us the salesmen weren't selling a lot but he was agoing ahead and

(Left to right) Customer A. M. Bynum, Coffeeville, Kansas, and three Warren Sewell Clothing Company employees: Warren Sewell, Ed Morris, James Pollard—March 1964.

give us work. He was that kind of man. He made suits and put 'em back and they'd sell 'em later and maybe lose money on them, but yet he give us a hand, he kept us going.''

In keeping his plant open he kept his employees at work, and so maintained their payroll and their confidence in his business. He took a risk in doing this, especially with regard to the large inventory stock. His wish to do these things and to sell, to move the goods, led him into various clothing trials—into topcoats, boys' clothing, car coats—but he remained hitched to his prime resource, to men's suits and sport coats.

One of his plant managers suggested once that they build a new plant, really fix it up to be first class. His response was "No, the people we sell to don't give a durn if we make it in a blacksmith shop."

The third component in Sewell's vision of the clothing business was getting and keeping workers. He had strong ideas about work and work expectations. He was convinced of the necessity and beauty of work. A Sewell worker for decades said of him: "He believed in work. If you worked, if you tried, he was for you. That's all you had to do, just try."

An official who began with the company at age twenty-two said: "Mr. Sewell believed in hard work, in an out-of-the-ordinary way. He worked all the time and expected others to. He was not demanding, but he expected you to work, to keep out of trouble, and to produce." Said a bank director: "He wanted a day's work for a day's pay. He wanted you to have everything that was coming to you and he wanted everything that was coming to him."

Though no slave driver, he expected hard work and would say, "Hired for five days' work, not to drink soda pop." He had no patience with people who wasted time. As a woman supervisor said, "He believed in working, he didn't believe in loafing."

Even as he was earnest about work and opposed to any frivolous approach to it, he was not grim or deadly about it. At one time the stockroom was in an old cotton warehouse that had a rough wooden floor from which the workers secured many splinters. One of them said, "Mr. Warren, we need a new floor. Just look here. I'm getting tired of getting splinters in my shoes." He did not respond but soon returned from Wilson Clothing Company with a big smile and a pair of heavy thick-soled country brogans for each of them.

His ideas about hiring and about retirement were deep seated, rooted in his country origin. He stated frequently that the west Georgia, east Alabama area was one of the best in the country because it was filled with people who would work. Again and again he told his workers that they were the salt of the earth.

When he responded "Yes, Momma" to his mother's suggestion that he hire someone from the neighborhood, he felt this acquiescence involved little risk. Explained a resident: "People in this area have an idea of work. He'd hire workers if they were willing, for in Graham and Woodland people still believe in work." He felt farm people were unspoiled for good work and that people too close to big industry were not good bets.

A worker from Woodland, Alabama, commented on the success of the Sewell search for a community-oriented, family-oriented, productive enterprise. He pointed to the value of the industry itself and of the leadership bringing it there, but also to the importance of "the kind of people who were here to be helped." These good working people constituted the precious ingredient Warren Sewell sought when he moved from the city to Bremen.

Frequently people who worked for Warren Sewell did not speak of being hired, but of "being taken in," in the sense of one allowed into a lodge or into a fraternal order. As one employee remarked, "I think Mr. Warren's greatest desire about the company was that we work together as a family unit. He took my wife in and not only that he took my son in, and he's done that for many families. It's a family affair."

In hiring Warren Sewell made up his mind quickly and stuck with his decisions. "He didn't make many mistakes on this," said one employee, "no, he didn't. I tell you he was quite a man on that. Like I tell you, he wanted the background. He always wanted to know where you came from and what kind of family you came from. If you were a family man and your family was pretty well known and assessed, he'd hire you."

He sometimes hired people based on their physical agility, their sense of action. One of his supervisors recounted

Warren Sewell and his employees, Bowdon, Georgia, plant, June 1959.

that Sewell saw a young fellow laying brick, moving fast and working hard, and hired him right then as a shipping clerk.

Many people began working for him as teenagers and continued into their eighties; never working for anyone else. Others were thirty-five, forty, or fifty when he hired them. He had an enlightened view of the responsibilities of a businessman and hired even older people who wanted work and perhaps should not have been working so late in life. He paid them regular wages, and if they were untrained he found a job for them. In his judgment he got good employees that way.

Once on a Sunday he and his wife Ava were out driving through the hilly Alabama countryside and stopped to talk to a seventy-five-year-old woman, plowing on the Sabbath. He offered her a job, and she came to work. When the supervisor protested to Warren Sewell that her hands were too crippled with arthritis for her to use the sewing needle, he replied that he was to find her a job in the stockroom or somewhere else.

One of his supervisors said he protested to Warren Sewell about this practice now and then, pointing out the practical problems of aged employees, to no avail.

In addition to hiring workers and offering work and honest treatment, he let employees work as long as they wanted. He considered it a waste when a well-trained, devoted, and capable worker stopped work.

He never asked anyone to retire. He shifted people to other jobs sometimes, such as out of the sewing room if that work was dangerous to them. When Jimmie Witt, a worker who had been a neighbor since childhood as well as a schoolmate, grew older and could not remember, a supervisor had her go home. As soon as Warren Sewell heard of this, he sent for her, bringing her back to the plant and assuring her that she had a job. There is no record of what he said to the supervisor, if anything. But for Jimmie Witt, there was dignified work until she decided to retire. All during his lifetime there were numbers of older women on regular jobs in the plant.

There was no retirement pay, no Social Security. But an old-time employee pointed out: "Never anyone lost their job for age." Eventually the firm instituted a program for modest retirement pay. One of the first to draw such pay proudly said: "I draw fifty dollars a month as long as I live. We didn't pay into it. He thought about us way back."

Warren Sewell had some firm ideas about working hours. He liked people to be on the job early in the mornings, saying that when a man was rested, his mind was rested, and he could produce for himself and benefit the company. The worker commenting added that "he's a man I met in the morning, time after time, going down to his farm to supervise it. I was coming in to the plant to work—in the summertime it was at seven o'clock—but he was ahead of me. He practiced what he preached." Today the plant whistle still goes off early, at eight in the morning.

He believed in the early hours. John Cook said, "He lived down below me. About daylight he'd be out going to the farm or to the plant or to Atlanta, and me on my way to the shop. 'John,' he'd say, 'what do you know that I ought to know?'" One worker thought Warren Sewell surely must have spent the early hours getting the multitude of notes and papers in his coat straightened out.

When Warren Sewell was working in the plant and wanted to go to his nearby Graham farm, he went. But if afterwards he came in to the plant at 4:30 on Saturday, he expected his workers to be there.

"Sometimes," one supervisor recollected, "we had so many thousand suits we had to make between the seasons that I'd have to work at night. I worked lots and lots at night. Back when we made overcoats we didn't have machinery to operate both suits and topcoats at the same time, and I'd run the coat factory during the day and the topcoats at night. No overtime, you worked by the piece or the day."

In the stockroom they worked late when there were special orders to get out. Railway Express and the truck lines ran on Saturday afternoon, and if a merchant called in at 4 p.m.

John Cook.

on Saturday with a special need, no matter how small or large, Warren Sewell said get it out that day.

Another worker noted: "Nearly as long as he lived, we stayed open six days a week through Saturday. The only change we've made is that we close now at noon on Saturday. Some of the plants don't open on Saturday at all."

In the plant there was no Sunday work except perhaps for boiler repair. Absolutely no manufacturing, sewing, or selling on Sunday. No merchants were allowed in on the Sabbath. All that was permitted was keeping the machinery up.

Once the stockroom crowd had to work all night Saturday getting a large order out, but when the sun came up on Sunday they went home. Only when there was a death in a local family and someone needed a suit for the funeral did the stockroom open on Sunday.

Employees had a week's vacation, and the stockroom people staggered their time off. But one year Warren Sewell closed up the stockroom and gave them all the same week off. A week without the shipping department to respond to special customer needs led some merchants to feel Mr. Sewell had died and the plant had been shut down. This was the end of the experiment.

The plant was open not only on Saturdays but also on New Year's Day, and one commentator said Warren Sewell would have kept open on the Fourth of July if he could have, adding: "But he never asked anyone to do anything he wouldn't do himself. He was always there and always working."

His own example was important. He combined personal commitment with authority, an authority flowing not from discipline but from his personality and the standards of work and behavior that he exemplified.

A Bremen resident said of him: "He pulled people along well. None of the Sewells were well-educated men but they were brilliant people. They didn't understand anything but work. They never thought about taking a vacation or anything like that until they got pretty wealthy."

A career employee said that in her four decades of work, she never had to ask for a raise. "Mr. Warren always seen, you know, that these things come along, he was that good. We didn't have to beg for a raise or anything." She added: "When I went to work at Warren Sewell Clothing Company you know how much money I made, three dollars a week. And I worked many a day and it was nearly dark walking home. I didn't get overtime, but we had repairs and I didn't mind helping get 'em straightened out. I worked, yessiree, but back then you could buy a pork chop probably for a nickel, eggs 8 to 10 cents a dozen."

Warren Sewell's employees were free-spirited, independent people, of farming or small town stock. Bound together on prolonged and interrelated work in somewhat confined physical surroundings, one would expect there to be disciplinary problems, some physical outbursts, disagreements, fights. There were few. Thoughtfulness and mutual good manners were more the norm. Company policy assisted in this objective, for if a worker fought in the plant, he got fired. If the scrappers were good men, they would usually be taken back to work after a month or two.

A veteran sewing-room supervisor for Warren Sewell said that in all her years, she never had to carry forward a disciplinary problem. "I treated the boys and girls like I'd like to be treated. I put them in my place. I never did have any trouble with any of them, having to send them to the office for anything." The nearest came when she first began such work and had a young man and woman working next to each other, pressing side seams. When she was rearranging their work spaces to give both sufficient room, the young man became angry and said to his supervisor: "Goddammit, if you don't like it, press 'em yourself."

Knowing he'd be fired if she reported the matter, she made no formal report. However, he was married to another plant employee, a good friend of hers, to whom she spoke of his behavior. By the time it was over, the fellow probably wished the supervisor had merely reported him and had him fired.

Once a man was caught stealing suits, throwing them out the window to a confederate who made off with them. The employee was tried, found guilty, and sentenced. Warren Sewell told him that when he got out and came back, he would rehire him.

Similarly, when he discovered that a farmer working for him on his place had stolen half his crop, instead of firing him he put him back to work. Why not fire him and hire somebody else? His response was that if he hired a new man, he'd probably have to endure the same stealing process, while this fellow probably will not steal anymore, now that he had been caught.

The training and education of workers who had done no manufacturing before was a challenge. It was a great jump from the farm field to the production line for people who had been independent, who all their lives could stop and go as they pleased. They had plowed their own fields, cut their own hay, run their own lives. It took discipline and training for these people to get organized, to fit into the routine of the assembly line. Providing the training—and this entailed not merely technical training—was itself a difficult task.

Therefore, Warren Sewell picked people from families that he knew, figuring that for this reason he did not have to check on their background. He knew that they could be trained to do certain things. He would start them in the plant at something they could do, and from there he would move them up as they were capable of taking more responsibility.

At first he had a college graduate checking suits as they came off the line, then made him responsible that the stripes in the sleeves and body matched. Later, he moved him to the cutting room, where suits were cut to salesmen's orders.

Especially in the sales area where he himself worked, he taught by example. Said one retired salesman: "He had less formal education than I did and taught me more than I could ever have learned in Harvard."

The need for training and trained workers was always in his mind. One of his staff, Roy Davis, was telling how Warren Sewell could always make money on a deal, always come out ahead, never get stuck. He went with him one time, right after the Bremen-Bowdon Investment Company was started, to a bankrupt pants factory, one that did contract work.

Warren Sewell did not have a pants factory then. The owner knew Sewell wanted to buy his plant, and after Davis and Lamar Plunkett took inventory, it was apparent that his price was high. Nevertheless, Sewell accepted the seller's offer at once.

Davis was surprised, saying to himself that at last the boss has been stuck on a deal. Just then Warren Sewell casually secured the bankrupt owner's assurance of assistance in Sewell's company employing his trained work force. "I then remembered," said Davis, "that machinery was scarce, but that trained workers were more so."

As to education Warren Sewell told one of his salesmen once: "You know, a man don't go to school to get an education to work for himself. He goes to school to work for a man who doesn't have an education." When after the Korean War his son wanted to continue college and get an MBA, he opposed it, saying he should be the salesman and hire somebody to do those other things.

James Pollard, an accountant who became credit manager, had been to West Georgia College and the University of Georgia. Warren Sewell told him that he was hiring him in spite of his schooling.

A few of his plant's technical people were sent off for training. Eula Norton went to New York to learn all she could about sewing-room operation and about making coats and suits. Cliff Hughes, Jr. went there to find out how to make coats that fit. Twice Cole Bell was sent to Richmond to Friedman Marks Clothing Company to learn how to implement new pressing-room techniques, including how to press coat sleeves round.

An important ingredient of Warren Sewell's plant operation was his own accessibility to his workers. He was a good friend to everyone. People were not afraid to talk to him. Said one of his staff associates: "He made himself available to people who maybe never had much attention. He was interested in people."

An employee spoke of his availability: "If anybody wanted to come in and see him, ok, the door was open, didn't matter who you were, you could come right in and talk. The workers perceived him as one of their own. He grew up on a farm and knew how to cut fodder and hay and raise grain and cattle. When you went in to see him, you could communicate with him. He acted like he was real glad to see you and asked you were your turnip greens up yet. He would help you resolve your problems."

Access to him was easy. The workers did not have to go to his office. Explained a plant manager: "He could be walking through the plant and somebody would stop him and say 'I need help, my family's ill' or 'I need help on my house.' 'Why, all right, I'll call the bank, and if you haven't got a way to get there, I'll send you.' And he'd expect you to go. The people in the plant knew this, and they knew he'd help. They knew they would be comfortably received. He was one of

them, they'd started together, and from the plow lines upward they felt bound all together with him."

Another employee, a supervisor, added, "If you went to
him for help, he never turned you down." One did not always need to ask for help, however. An Atlanta banker noted:
"If he knew of someone in need, he didn't go to them personally and hand it to them, but he saw they were taken care
of. I think that's the reason they felt that way about Mr. Warren. They knew he had a lot of compassion."

He reached out to help his workers. One of the first
things he tried to do for a young man he hired was get him
in the Masons. The next thing was to get him some life insurance. Said one employee: "Now he believed in people
having life insurance. Every boy came in here he'd call the
life insurance man. We weren't making much money, but he
saw that the policy got paid. He encouraged them to get in
the Masons, and when you got through he bought you a pin
with a diamond in it. I have mine still, got it years ago."

He believed in communicating with his workers, speaking with them individually and in groups. "Well, he was nice
to all of us," said one. "If he had anything he'd call us together and tell us what was going to take place, and what kind
of changes he's going to make and everything. Sure was fair."

His son noted that his father enjoyed these talks to the
workers: "He was never happier than when talking to people
at the plant. The Christmas talks I especially remember." The
plant workers were much affected by these talks. One recalled a depression-era meeting of the workers:

> The whole country and the plant was down at a pretty low ebb.
> And it didn't look good for us by any means. And our sales were
> very low. I shall never forget Mr. Sewell. He stepped up to the
> platform, and he calmed the whole atmosphere of the people
> with every word he said. He said we're not broke yet. He gave
> the people something to look forward to, knowing he was going
> to stand out for them, work for them.

His individual contacts with workers were equally effective. A supervisor, ill in the Georgia Baptist Hospital with a

kidney infection and concerned about her job, was heartened when he visited her and told her to stop worrying: "I've got my shoes in your tracks while you're gone." Lois Waddell, whose husband had worked with a mule and a scoop shovel to rebuild the burned-out Bremen plant, said: "Warren Sewell depended on my husband's opinion, and Lee thought him the best friend he ever had." Perhaps this comment from her summed up the general worker's view: "He perhaps had some slack points, but as far as we who worked for him, we never saw them."

A retired couple, both of whom had worked much of their lives in the plant, concurred in their assessment: "We can't say nothing against Mr. Sewell. Everything we know is good."

For decades Warren Sewell kept his plant open and operating; seldom was it at a lowered manpower level for any reason, be it seasonal change, lack of sales, or union threat. Said a woman employee of many years' service about the union question: "Well, I think Mr. Warren's attitude toward his people and the provisions he made for the people was OK, he kept us working and we had something to do. And he would work hard to keep everything going so that things would run smooth, so his people would not lose earnings. To me that's the whole story."

An employee of long service, now retired, gave his explanation of the union matter: "Mr. Warren handled the union by treating people well and letting them know he trusted them. He surely did, let me tell you. And he'd never call over here and say you wouldn't have a job if you voted for the union. That wasn't his way of doing business. You voted like you wanted to, but he always come out on top. He didn't always pay more, he was just a good businessman, and everybody had confidence in him and in working at Warren Sewell Clothing Company. I tell you there wasn't but very few days that Warren Sewell Clothing Company didn't operate."

Both Warren Sewell and his workers were of the soil, attuned to farm life, to small town living. They were church- and family-oriented. He was not essentially different from his workers in any way. He knew about family problems, for he had an extended family and many responsibilities, of which his workers well knew.

He attended the same church, went to the same sing-ings, buried his family members and theirs in the same churchyard, prayed aloud in church for himself and for them. He dressed as they did, and when he worked on his farm in rubber boots and rough clothing, he looked like any other farmer.

His workers had complete accessibility to him, on a di-rect and informal basis. They knew their reception would be

(Left) Riddley Lovvorn; (right) Warren Sewell, about 1943.

comfortable, for he always demonstrated an instant compassion and genuine interest in them and their problems.

A plant manager offered a key to understanding Sewell, his workers, and the union. Long ago the manager himself had been personally recruited by Sewell, who observed him as a young man at vigorous work in the field. The manager explained that it was the plow lines of their rural origin that bound Warren Sewell and his country-based workers together in mutual understanding. "People so bound," he said, "made good producers—in worker, in supervisor, in owner. It was the plow lines that always beat the union."

A worker got to the heart of it by noting, "Mr. Warren felt he could do better for us than the union, and we felt this also. He didn't always pay us as much as the union, generally but not always. He took care of us. But in the end it's because he didn't want it. This is the reason, not anything else." Another said: "We sure didn't want it if he didn't. We didn't just depend on him for work, we depended on him for life, and he on us." When union efforts first began, there were some workers who were interested and wanted the union, but as one put it: "There wasn't many after they found out what Mr. Warren felt about it."

A retired salesman who began as a stockroom clerk in Atlanta said: "Mr. Sewell never did tell me he disliked the union. But I knew he did, and he had something better to offer. He proved it every day; he treated us well. You know, a lot of places you worked you were numbers, but in Warren Sewell Clothing Company he knew your name." Another reported: "He had a sense of feeling and respect for the people who worked for him. The people who work at the plant are family more than they are just business associates."

He did not like the unions, considering them a disservice to the country. He could see no good in them, and he decried their organizing efforts as blatant and self-serving rabble-rousing.

He was well advised on labor and personnel matters. Not only did he have his local legal firm, but he also employed an Atlanta labor-law firm. The local firm kept up with union efforts and plans very well. Indeed, the union had little success in documenting any anti-labor or plant-closing threats by him.

He had strong feelings, and he did not have to have his private say but once. His workers understood his opposition to the union, which he conveyed in a variety of fashions, most of them quite indirect. They would hear that a worker had spoken to him about the union "working on us again," and that he sighed and said, "Looks like we're gonna have to close the plant till further notice."

They knew he fully owned the plant, carried the key, and had repeatedly said, "If I want to shut that door I don't have to ask nobody." They also knew Warren Sewell had said they could have a union if they wished one; however, he added that he would not operate with a union and would close up. They knew it and they believed it. "It was his personal appeal," said one employee, "and the people thinking he'd do the best he could to keep the plant going, would pay as much as he could. They believed him, that he'd have closed."

A white-haired retired woman worker, her arthritic hands worn from sewing, said: "Unions? He hated 'em, and so did I. He didn't believe in, you know, unions. He said he wouldn't work under a union at all. And we never did sign up for it either. He was a good old fellow. I don't think you could have had a better boss man nowheres than he was."

An Atlanta banker put it simply: "He didn't have much time for the union. He didn't need much. Faith was the key to his success. His workers had faith and implicit confidence that he knew what he was doing. They trusted him, and he didn't have to go through the process of selling his people on himself."

Observed grocer Will Roop: "Of course Warren didn't like the union. But he got along, and his people never did want to organize. I don't think they had the slightest desire to. They always felt they were part of the plant."

At that time the laws about labor and unions were not very strict. Neither were the unions well organized nor especially competent in their organizing efforts. There was a small and quiet union in a shirt shop in Bremen. And there were efforts at organizing the clothing plants in the Bremen area, including those belonging to Warren Sewell. Against some plants in the area there were repeated efforts. But with the several votes held in the Warren Sewell Clothing Company plants, the union lost every time, often by very large margins.

Once when the cutting room was rearranged, there was a brief sit-down of 245 workers at the Bowdon plant. An injunction was quickly issued; the sheriff came from his nearby, familiar office and spoke about good behavior. There was neither threat nor promise. The workers went home and promptly returned to work.

A local banker commented that the union tried repeatedly, then gave up. He pointed out that Warren Sewell paid a higher wage scale, treated his workers well, gave them vacations and time off when needed, and had a flexibility that the union never had. He could be a step ahead all the way, and his employees were intensely loyal.

As with any other clothing manufacturer, Warren Sewell had the problem of following trends and fashion and altering his clothing style. A longtime supplier of cloth who was in touch with the Warren Sewell Clothing Company for many years spoke of the firm's view of fashion and style. "The nature of their business was to follow the strong trends. They were never fashion originators. They picked the best things in the market, what the marketplace wanted, and gave it to their customers at a very, very low price. I don't say cheap. They sold the working man's very popularly priced clothing, and that's not style-innovative. They stayed abreast of the trends very well, being out in the marketplace all week long, every week."

One of the retailers out in the marketplace talked about how Warren Sewell would visit with him. "He'd ask me about various suits, styles, colors, how they were moving. What do you think would be a good prospect for another year? Are they going to sell next year? He kept his finger on the market all the time."

Warren Sewell had certain key merchants that he leaned on for information about what was selling. They would send him garments, expensive goods that they had bought elsewhere. He would also see in the stores what he wanted and liked. He and his stylist would study all these items, then copy and adapt them. For popularly priced business this procedure was best, for the popular items would usually be one or two years behind the top lines. He listened, he absorbed what he heard. He had a lot of knowledge and input from the marketplace. He hewed to medium conservative clothes, including young men's clothing.

Occasionally the firm developed new lines through its own processes, as one employee pointed out: "Mr. Plunkett, he wanted to make sport coats. He had been in the service and he knew a lot and he felt like sport coats were coming and sure enough they did, and we had sport coats."

Warren Sewell was a listening man. He talked with his own salesmen and listened to the cloth salesmen. He visited mills, always asking the stylist and the salesman what the coming thing was for the season. For style and fashion change he depended on what he heard and saw.

Lamar Plunkett recounted making his first mill visit with Warren Sewell in the 1940s. They went to American Mills—"they were giants in those days, now gone"—to see Mr. Leecroft, who was the credit man. "Mr. Sewell always wanted to see the credit man and ask about money and what was going to happen to it."

When he came to the salesroom, he entered in a lightning hurry and would never take a seat. He would tell the salesman he was in a hurry, had an appointment down the road, and wanted to see the salesman's two best numbers. (To Plunkett he privately said that when you are in a hurry, the salesman thinks you have money and is therefore ready to sell.)

Plunkett explained: "You know what the man would do, he'd go get 'em. He'd select them, for he knew them and he knew what sold. Mr. Sewell didn't look through a pile of stuff this high. If he liked the two numbers, he'd say, 'These are nice looking, let me see your next two best sellers.' The sales-man would want to add a few more, but he would train him and say no. Then he'd buy at the drop of a hat. He'd say, 'I'll take these two numbers and I'll take fifty pieces of each, 4,000 yards each, and that's what I'll do, and I want you to ship them right away.' He had the fellow in his pocket, and next season when he showed up that salesmen knew he'd better get his best goods out or Warren Sewell would be gone." In this fashion he generally saw the best numbers in every mill he visited.

Eventually almost all the firm's cloth purchases, per-haps ninety percent, were made in Bremen, from salesmen who came to them. For special transactions such as the large Belk's order Sewell would travel to New York, or would take a trip just to shop the market. He personally bought all the basic materials but not the trimmings.

Not only could Warren Sewell buy, he could sell. In re-sponse to a question about the central reason for the success of Warren Sewell, a Bremen friend and competitor said, "He sold and he made other folks sell all the time, so skip all the rest. He was a salesman." A Bremen banker said succinctly, "Warren could sell sunshine in August."

He viewed the production and sale of a suit as an act of supreme masculine accomplishment. He took great pleasure in the transaction, the bargain arrived at over the suit. When he sold it and the customer wore it, everything else became of lesser importance. That suit and every other one in his life, including those he wore, meant a great deal to him, but not as adornment or dress. It was the consummate pleasure of a bargain arrived at, one that ended by being beneficial to both the producer and consumer.

His nephew, Ray Sewell, Sr., also a clothing manufac-turer, saw Warren's first capacity as sales, then productivity, and third finance and credit. "He possessed great wisdom in all these, and I'd say more of his wisdom was in selling than in producing. But he had somebody willing who knew how to get it out, good enough to sell, and at a price that was sell-able."

"He was not," said Jack Worley, "a numbers man or an organizer. He depended on other people for those things. He was primarily a salesman, a good one." One of his salesmen said, "He loved people and he loved the clothing business. He'd rather sit down and sell clothes than eat."

His philosophy was that he would never say no to the prospective customer. He would find some way to keep the transaction going. If the question was do you have so and so in the house and he did not have it, he never answered directly, but said, "This might be better or I can get it for you. You give me an order and I'll send it." The customer might eventually get something else, but he would probably like it as well or better. Lois Waddell spoke for all the plant employees when she termed Warren Sewell "the one and only salesman."

A longtime salesman for the firm described Warren Sewell's selling success as follows: "Warren Sewell had personality and he knew the territory and he knew his product, from top to bottom and side to side. He knew everything about the suit. And he knew his customer—his needs, his credit limits, and his personality. You can't beat that combination. He was ahead of the customer. He could glance at his clothing racks and say what the fellow needed. And he'd lay it out on the table and tell him why he needed it."

A salesman told of traveling with Warren Sewell once: "He'd sometimes buy some of the trashiest old piece goods in the world. One time I was traveling with him in South Carolina and he had this old stack of swatches, stuff he couldn't get rid of. We were going through the different price ranges for a customer, and for every range Mr. Warren would put the old swatches on top. Finally the fellow said, 'Mr. Warren, I'll take some of this. It must be a good piece of goods, you've got it in every price range.' After the order was written, I picked up the sample case, and when we got in the car, Mr. Warren said, 'Now see what you boys make me do. You all won't sell them dogs, I have to sell 'em.' "

Warren Sewell was an expert at getting rid of inventory. A retailer recalled how he kept his plant open, "ran it even though he just broke even. While he usually had a market for what he made, when it was necessary he could get on the phone and sell more merchandise than half his sales force together. He might have to shave the price a little, but he could move it. He would phone his old-time customers—Rich's or Parks-Chambers or someone in Louisville or Knoxville—telling them he had merchandise that was not moving and wished to send them so many thousand suits on consignment. 'Take 'em and send back what won't sell,' he'd say. But they wouldn't send back too many. That's how he unloaded stock."

Warren Sewell was close to his customers and saw and talked with them frequently. For instance, he was very friendly with the men at Belk's, a large Southern department store, with Ralph Clemmer and with Mr. Craig, who was the buyer. He also had good relations with the people in the D. C. Wright Clothing Company store of Greensboro, North Carolina. He was out there in the marketplace every day, and being there gave him a good grasp of this facet of his business.

He was receptive to a supplier who wished to sell to him. He was a salesman himself and probably a lot easier to convince than one who was not. Herb Avery, salesman for a firm that was a large supplier of cloth to Warren Sewell Clothing since 1946, said: "He was a great salesman. One of the things that interested me was how we salesmen had to spend most of our Saturdays in Bremen because of Mr. Warren. He traveled, he was on the road from Monday through Friday, and if you wanted to sell him, you better get out there on Saturday. If you missed him on Saturday, that was it. Sunday was reserved for God and Pastor Louie Newton."

From years of visiting Bremen, staying there, and knowing and observing the clothing business and the interesting people in it, the salesmen sometimes termed Bremen "Peyton Place with a Christian atmosphere."

One retailer, a customer of Warren Sewell for thirty-five years, spoke of Warren's relationship with customers, large and small. This fellow had a small store and said when he

Pastor Louie D. Newton and Warren Sewell, 1953.

came to the Warren Sewell Clothing Company, he would get the few suits he needed and be going. He could see that Warren Sewell was busy, "sitting there in that office about where Ed Morris is now, except they've cut it up some. One day he stopped me and asked why I was not coming in to see him. 'Mr. Sewell, I figured you were busy and got no time to spend with a little cottonpicker like me.' He told me, 'You are the ones I get my information from. I just wouldn't know anything that was going on if I didn't have somebody like you and the other merchants to get my information from. I'm not out there retailing, I'm making it, and I got to know what's going on.' "

Lamar Plunkett recalled, "When he'd meet someone from New York, he'd say, 'Tell me, Good Friend'—that was his remark to everyone—'Tell me, Good Friend, what I should know that you know.' They would tell him, and he would winnow it within his mind."

With Warren Sewell Clothing Company salesmen all over the country, there were many customers that only the salesmen saw. The plant employees talked to them by phone but never met them. Occasionally merchants would come from far away, just to see the plant and meet their telephone contacts.

Not only did Warren Sewell stay in touch with his customers, small or large, he was evenhanded in his treatment of them. Accordingly, he asked his salesmen to be equally fair. A longtime salesman said: "You could be the smallest merchant in the state and we were to treat you well and like everyone else. Mr. Warren had us treat all the same, whether they're buying two or three suits or a lot. They all got the same treatment. For the same item of clothing we sold it to the smallest merchant for the same price as we did to the big department store."

In one city frequently there would be the same Sewell fleece flannel sport coat, with three different private labels, selling for $12.75 in one store, for $24.50 in another, and for more than $30 in the third.

His salesmen were constrained as to price shaving. They sold the same thing at the same price everywhere, always with the hope that the firm had mixed the price and the quality correctly.

Warren Sewell was renowned for being expert at this balance. A plant executive outlined a case: "I think it was back in 1950 he came out with an all wool, flannel, charcoal grey suit. It was the rage. They had a sales meeting and Mr. Warren said, 'Boys, I've got you something you can really get out there and sell. I've got an all wool, charcoal grey suit, and the price is $19.75.' One of the salesmen spoke up and asked how he could sell that suit for that price. 'Boys, you just go out there and sell 'em, I'll find a way to squeeze some profit out of them.' And he would, he knew what he was doing."

For a customer who ordered ahead of time the Warren Sewell Clothing Company would hold his clothing, though it was not paid for, for a reasonable time and not let anyone else have it. Sometimes these orders were held, from first cutting to shipping, for six months.

In selling he was as fair to customers as he could be, and they had confidence in him. A lot of customers would let him write their orders, feeling he knew what he was doing. They sensed that he knew what they needed when he walked in the store and looked at the racks. He knew more than the merchant did, including what he was selling and what most of the people were calling for, whereas the merchant knew just the area he was serving. In writing such an order for a customer, he would not load him up with $100,000 worth of suits if he didn't have the right area or the experience to move them.

In the stockroom where merchants came in to choose their purchases, there was a quietly established protocol. Arriving merchants were served in the order of their arrival. When one came in looking to buy two or three suits, he was cared for in his turn, notwithstanding the presence of another customer, a potential buyer of 500-600 suits. The stockroom manager explained that Warren Sewell was emphatic that the three-suit fellow be cared for in his turn.

Model Books of Warren Sewell Clothing Company.

Warren Sewell was known for his ability to handle customer problems and to simultaneously wield his "selling steam shovel." His son recalled how an occasional customer would call his father, "so mad he could spit nails" over receiving a shipment containing some flawed merchandise. By the time they were finished talking the customer's problem had been solved, his anger appeased, and he had placed a new order.

Warren Sewell could be firm with customers who took advantage. He would buy a good bargain in off-price piece goods, fine quality, make a bunch of suits and offer them at an attractive price. The company sold good worsted suits for $20. He always said, "I'll make my own and we'll have the best quality."

He had several accounts that would carry hundreds of these suits, keep them a long time, and return them if they did not sell. Some of his staff felt some firms took a little advantage of this liberal policy, but Warren Sewell did not look at it like that, as the customer was always right. But finally when his patience was tried, he wrote eight or ten of these firms, explaining why he had to close their account. Every one of them came back later.

Warren Sewell had the ability to take young people with no technical knowledge or training and place them in demanding jobs in which they did well. Generally they remained with him for years, bound by a sense of both affection and business accomplishment.

As a close associate of his commented: "People reared in that day, especially in the rural area around Bremen, had no light to see by, no example before them. Mr. Warren did not stand in awe of what he called big money or big operations, and he lit some fires within their minds, gave them some powers within themselves that they previously didn't have. He took farm boys—and I mean those reared on a farm, with little education—and sent them as salesmen to different parts of the country. And most did well, some unbelievably well."

Most began modestly. One graduate of the stockroom went somewhat reluctantly to another state to sell, leaving his wife in Georgia. Warren Sewell gave his wife a check for $50 each week and sent him $75, paying him a bonus at year's end. After a couple of years on a salary and expense account, Warren Sewell gave him the territory, had him move his family there, and furnished the down payment on a house.

The salesman explained: "Mr. Warren said, 'Now if you get hungry, call me.' And I stayed there twenty-seven years and never had a letter from Mr. Warren saying I had the territory, or anything about the job I was doing. When I saw him, he'd just say I was doing a good job."

Warren Sewell's criteria for selecting salesmen? Lamar Plunkett said: "He was big on family, on character, and pretty good on stick and performance. He paid awfully well." His salesmen worked strictly on commission, with credit given them for any mail or phone orders coming in from their territory.

In reality Warren Sewell raised most of his salesmen, taking them primarily from the stockroom. Some came from the membership of his church, Druid Hills Baptist, and several of these did remarkably well, caring for sales in a state and eventually moving and settling there.

He was unselfish about his salesmen. He wanted them to succeed, wanted them to make money, on a proper basis and through hard work. He considered himself a good judge of human nature and told them he did not want a man who could not earn at least $25,000 a year. He gave them two years. If they were not that successful he did not fire them but suggested they ought to find something else to do.

A retired salesman said that the personalism associated with Warren Sewell was correct. "It's a true picture. It's not false. He had a feeling for people that few have. In my case anything I have I owe to him. He gave me a chance. Oh, I had to work, you understand. When I was on the road I worked six days a week." He went on to say that in forty-one years of selling, Saturday was his biggest sales day.

His largest customer bought only on Saturday. He went to see the buyers late Friday, presented his line, and they would pick out what they liked. The rest he would stack in

Warren Sewell in a sales meeting, Carrollton Hotel, Carrollton, Georgia, about 1953.

the aisles, according to price, and Saturday morning they would go through it again, then have lunch. "In the twenty-five years I sold to this company, they never let me buy lunch one time."

After lunch he went back to the hotel, sometimes waiting till Sunday evening for them to call, so he could write the order. "It was always a good one, and I could have lived well off this one account for twenty-five years."

Salesmen who became ill or went into the service continued to draw their commission on sales made in their territory. The company paid the replacement salesman.

In 1945 when the Warren Sewell Clothing Company first began, salesmen made no calls, as garments were so scarce they were merely allotted by territory. For a year and a half his salesmen did not travel at all but drew their commission nevertheless.

Every Christmas he gathered the stockroom and other related employees together and would tell them that this year the company made a little money and he wanted them to have some of it. "He always gave us a bonus at Christmas, and the employees looked for this to buy our family presents."

In 1955 a salesman, traveling on salary and expenses, was at the gathering and was disappointed that he did not receive an envelope. But Warren Sewell asked him into the office, telling him that his territory made a little money in the year and that he wanted to share it. The bonus check he handed him was for $4,800, more money than the salesman had ever had before at one time.

He was thoughtful of the salesmen on the road regarding their ties with Bremen and their desire for news. He wrote to them regularly, especially about staff who were ill or hospitalized.

Similarly, for the families of the salesmen who lived in Bremen, he could be equally thoughtful. One wife of a man who just started traveling recalled her surprise and gratitude one morning, answering a knock at the back door, in seeing Warren Sewell in farm clothes and with an armful of farm produce. "Come to see how the widow's doing, now that her husband is traveling." He exuded a friendly interest and assurance that she still remembers.

One salesman said Warren Sewell had "no key admonitions to salesmen. He led a Christian life above reproach and expected others to do the same. He never admonished."

While he expected his salesmen to sell, he carefully distinguished between salesman and customer. One salesman took a prospective customer who had no money to Bremen to meet Warren Sewell. "Usually you'd tell Mr. Warren this is a good Baptist and he's got credit." But the credit manager said the man was not a good risk, that he was broke. To give the fellow some clothes the salesman stood good for the account.

In two or three months the man put a bankrupt sign on his store, and the salesman went to Bremen to see Warren Sewell, since the firm had charged the unpaid $1,800 for clothing to his personal account. He explained what happened: "Mr. Warren looked across the desk, with those glasses hanging down, his hat on, and his tie pointing wrong and said, 'You know, I always knew you didn't go to school long enough. I'm going to educate you, and it's going to cost you $1,800 to get an education.' From then on I never guaranteed another account, even good Baptist or good Methodist."

One salesman, sent to a nearby state to sell, said the only guidance Warren Sewell gave him was: "All I want to see from you is orders. Don't call and give me the weather report because I'll turn on the radio and get that."

The salesmen viewed him as a great man and a Christian man whose behavior and life reflected his views. He told one salesman that he did not need a man working for him "that's going to go out there and get drunk every night. I can find plenty of men to work for me that want to do something with their money." The salesman added, "In other words, you pretty well stayed straight or you didn't work."

Warren Sewell was a singleminded individual, and he expected concentrated effort from his sales force. He did not want wives to travel with them.

He expected his salesmen to be truthful in what they told customers. This was a cardinal point with him. A salesman said: "When the salesman told a customer something, it better be the truth."

Nonetheless he was supportive of his salesmen and entirely behind them. Once one of them sold a merchant in a small town twelve wash-and-wear suits at $14.75, then grabbed his hat and crossed the street, where he sold another fellow who had never bought before 100 at the same price.

The first customer wrote complaining bitterly of the salesman's action, citing his own record over the years as a choice account. In fact he had bought little, taken over six months to pay, and had no basis for an exclusive on the Sewell line. Warren Sewell cancelled his account, writing that a man who buys twelve suits and takes six months to pay is not a special customer.

Occurrences like this heartened the salesmen and let the customers know Warren Sewell valued both customer and salesman. He frequently told his salesmen how much he valued them, saying: "Look, this company can't run without salesmen." They knew of this regard and reciprocated. One testified: "He stood behind his salesmen. He could work people and he could get the best out of people. If Warren Sewell ever called me in Mississippi and said I need you, I thought enough of that man that I'd a crawled from Mississippi to Bremen, Georgia."

·CHAPTER V·

Banking, Business, and Farming

Country banks and their operation interested Warren Sewell, and as a member of their boards of directors he gave much time to local banks and to their affairs. One of his closest friends, Will Roop, who grew up with him and who was himself a banker, stated that he never knew why Warren Sewell was caught up in banking, why he liked it so much. He went on to say that as Sewell struggled and put his company together, grew and solved his financial problems, "Warren got a pretty good insight about banking, and he figured he'd better join them."

This he did, as far as the local banks were concerned. Roop owned a controlling interest in the Commercial Bank in Bowdon, and Warren Sewell did business with his friend's bank, keeping the manufacturing money there, which never involved a very large balance. The weekly payroll envelopes were sent to Bremen. Until 1973 the envelopes contained cash, as Warren Sewell did not want to have a woman trying to cash a check in a grocery store.

Another of his friends, J. J. Mangham, who assisted him in his move from Atlanta to Bremen, was head of the Commercial and Exchange Bank of Bremen at the time it was incorporated. Warren Sewell did considerable business with this bank, which in particular provided outside capital during 1950-1954.

His third specific interest in local banks was in Canton. His wife Ava inherited from her father stock in the Bank of Canton and in the Canton Cotton Mill, and he kept a close eye on the operation of both organizations.

He was a stockholder in the three banks mentioned—in Bremen, Bowdon, and Canton—and served on the board of directors of each one. He was chairman of two of them at one time or another.

He was very loyal to the banks in which he owned an interest, though he did some business also with the other local organization, the Haralson County Bank (later named First National) of Buchanan. Warren Sewell frequently said that during the depression it was the only bank on the railroad line from Chattanooga to Griffin that remained open, and he thought he had better stick with it. He later lost some of his enthusiasm for the Buchanan bank and the town itself when a number of workers from Buchanan who had lost their jobs sued him. He did virtually no business with Carrollton banks.

In getting his business started in Atlanta and west Georgia and in keeping it going, he had some experience in running around from one little bank to another. Raymond Otwell, his financial man, said the firm had no long-term obligations, but a large number of short-term ones. "It took a lot of banks to stay solvent."

As his firm grew so did his banking connections, for he obtained substantial lines of credit with Trust Company of Georgia, First National of Atlanta, and Hanover of New York, and a smaller line with a Raleigh, North Carolina, bank. He

Board of Directors, Commercial Bank, Bowdon, Georgia, 1971.
(Front row): C. C. Ozier, Warren Sewell, W. C. Roop, Zelma B. Harman.
(Back row): M. L. Johnson, Sr., Lamar Plunkett, W. A. Bowman, Jr.

liked the Raleigh bank, as they did not take interest out in advance. His relations with Atlanta's Trust Company and First National were harmonious and long-lasting. He had a studied lack of interest in the C & S Bank of Atlanta, due to what he felt was the lack of understanding and the overzealous wish for security exhibited by a bank officer who was a member of his church. Warren Sewell walked away, took his business elsewhere, never went back, and never quit talking about it.

In general he depended on the New York firm for funds to pay bills for supplies and on local and regional banks for capital funds.

Warren Sewell considered his firm to be a town-developed activity, a local business. And he operated that way, providing a balance sheet for Dun and Bradstreet but no operating statement. "That's our money, and it ain't nobody else's business," he said. Once in a while Otwell took an audit to show a bank, but it always came back and went in the safe. The firm simply never put out operating figures to anyone, including clothing mills and bankers.

He believed business debt was all right, "provided you have the opportunity to pay back. I am more jealous of my credit than anything I ever had. I have never lost my credit."

In his personal life he avoided indebtedness, doing what he urged on his workers—stay out of debt. He told his son that the only thing he ever bought on time was a piano, used for lessons for his daughter Frances. "And I told myself if I ever get that thing paid for I'll never borrow on anything for my house again."

Warren Sewell insisted that at some time during each year the firm's account with each bank was to be completely paid up. He felt that it made a good impression on the bank to see a double red line drawn under his zero balance. Also it made the bank wonder if he really was coming back for more business.

Another business rule of his was never to take discounts for early payment of invoices. He felt that if he took the discount and got used to it, dependent on it, the privilege might

Board of Directors, Commercial and Exchange Bank, Bremen, Georgia, 1973.
(Front row, left to right): J. Peel Mangham, Sam W. Hubbard, J. S. McEachern, Sr.,
Warren Sewell, Sr., Roy B. Sewell, Sr., S. Otis Higgins.
(Back row, left to right): Clark R. Stapler, George W. Shelnutt, Jack Worley, Harold O. Higgins,
Roy B. Sewell, Jr., John S. Hubbard, Warren P. Sewell, Jr., James S. McEachern, Jr.

be withdrawn at a time when his firm needed the money. He would rather forgo the current reward so he would be sure he was prepared to meet the future obligation.

Warren Sewell enjoyed the country banking business, was a good director, helpful to both the board and to the officers of the bank. Faithful in attendance, he never missed a bank meeting day. He told his driver, Clyde Newell, "It's every second Monday in Canton, and you get me there." Frequently he traveled a thousand miles or so to get back for a directors' meeting.

At such meetings the cashier of one bank brought in to the directors the meeting materials, including an envelope on top containing their fee in cash. Warren Sewell always took his envelope and remarked: "You know, there's two bad paymasters—one that pays before the work's done, the other that never pays at all."

As to why a busy manufacturer would spend so much time on the details of rural banking, one of his fellow directors explained, "He liked to keep his finger in the pie, he liked to know what was going on. It was an outlet for him and an exercise in intelligence gathering." He enjoyed the people he met through bank gatherings and found the meetings a source of information and insight. Banks then had relatively more power and influence than they would later, and he relished his participation and valued the economic news he secured.

An Atlanta banker also noted that Warren Sewell "felt an obligation for the proper conduct of banking." While he believed in high standards for loans, he wanted the banks to serve and to assist the local population. He sent scores of his workers to the bank for help, on the houses they were buying, the children they were educating. Also, he sent advance word saying he hoped that bank could assist; if not, he knew of another bank.

On the appropriate occasion he repeated to the other bank directors the rule of the "Three P's": loan no money to painters, plumbers, or preachers.

Clyde (Buck) Newell,
Warren Sewell's driver, 1972.

When a church board wished a loan of $10,000 and all ten of them signed to secure it, one bank director wondered about the need for that many pledges. "In banking," Sewell said, "there's no such thing as too much security."

Once when the Canton bank was having troubles, the explanation given by a bank officer to the board of directors was that people were not borrowing, that there was difficulty in making loans. Warren Sewell promptly said he would assist by borrowing $25,000. The bank official mailed him a promissory note and, to his surprised indignation, a request for full security. Warren Sewell concluded the bank needed a new president, and secured permission from his banker friend J. J. Mangham in Bremen to send one of Mangham's employees, E. O. McFather, up to Canton to meet the bank's board members. McFather became president of the Canton bank.

When Warren Sewell first moved from Atlanta to Bremen, he had a reasonable and natural affinity for the general area. After all his birthplace was nearby with his parents' home still there, and Bowdon was the site of his schooling. With deliberation he drew his workers from the farms and the small towns nearby, not from towns that already had factory payrolls and union problems.

In doing this he passed over Carrollton, which was nearby, larger, more affluent, and more social. There was a Mandeville Mill plant in Carrollton. And in the Bowdon area there was a lingering feeling that the Georgia Board of Regents and Carrollton had worked together to close Bowdon College and shift its activity to Carrollton.

A Sewell plant employee gave her opinion about Warren Sewell and Carrollton as follows: "He come to Bremen, his place was Bremen. He come to Bowdon, his place was Bowdon. This was home for him. They had manufacturing in Carrollton."

One of his relatives explained Sewell's concentration of interest in Bremen and Bowdon like this: "You know a man can carry a 200-pound sack of fertilizer, but you can't put 400 on his other shoulder." In other words, Warren Sewell had

Lumber trucks, Bowdon, Georgia, early 1900s.

enough to do in the place where he had established responsibilities and sentimental ties, close to his Graham, Alabama,
wellsprings. He neither built plants in Carrollton nor did he
permit his interest in banking to draw him to Carrollton.

Many attribute to Warren Sewell wisdom in forecasting
business trends and in predicting the future capacity and
managerial skills of untried and untrained people. He had an
intuitive sense of future possibilities, a knack in judging people and seeing in them more than they themselves knew was
there. Of course, mixed with that he had a large measure of
good luck.

Some saw these characteristics as simply gifts of provi-
dence to a generous and deserving man. A frequent comment was that the Lord and Warren Sewell were on the same
wave length, or "I just always considered that the Lord knew
Warren Sewell was there." At the same time these testifiers
generally added that as he matured, he developed his insight
and learned more about judging people.

In his own climb from the furrow to manufacturing success he did it on his own, receiving little help. Knowing this,
he felt that if one tried and had the will power to do something, any fears and inadequacy could be overcome. What
was good for him could be good for others. He therefore gave
people tasks without worrying about whether they had the
capacity, without guiding them closely or setting restraints
or checks on them. He placed them on the path, and almost
all succeeded and assisted him to success also. "He was a
good judge of people," said one of his staff, "and he had the
ability of finding the spot where a man could do good."

When he began to put numerous salesmen on the road,
he dismantled the nationwide chain of company stores. Some
were closed, others sold to the operators, many of whom used
this business start to move forward to very profitable businesses. He was proud of every one of them.

In addition to these people Warren Sewell assisted many
small merchants to expand their businesses. One reported
about his start: "Warren Sewell had faith in me, confidence
in me to the extent that when nobody else would give me

Management and sales force, Warren Sewell Clothing Company, early 1950s.

credit, he gave me ninety days to pay, when his regular terms were thirty. That was more than thirty years ago. I am a one-hundred-percent Warren Sewell man."

One who knew him long and closely said: "I'll tell you what I believe one of Warren Sewell's secrets was, if there is such a thing as a secret: his wisdom in picking people out. I've heard him say a lot of times that so much as is in a man will come out, that success is ninety percent work and ten percent brains, that if a man was educated and had the willingness to learn, he could achieve what he wanted to do."

Warren Sewell's ability to judge men led him to give vigorous assistance to business acquaintances to establish clothing business ventures, the control and management of which were turned over to them. Here too he appeared never to have the impulse to retain any long-term check or restraint over people once he got them started in business for themselves.

Here, as with his staff, he saw himself in the young men of limited training and good character, and wished them to have opportunity, without restraint or wet nursing. He so loved being his own man that he did not wish to restrict others, feeling that he would thereby hinder the other fellow and diminish himself. He valued his own independence very highly.

One Bremen resident explained what he termed Warren Sewell's extraordinary willingness to assist Sam Hubbard to create his own company: "He took Sam under his wing because he felt he deserved the chance and because he and Sam shared the same kind of Christian beliefs."

Warren Sewell maintained this respect toward others' independence both for business acquaintances and for family members. In the family he provided to those who sought it encouragement, financial assistance, a free range to run. Sometimes these ventures were successful, sometimes not.

His son said of this family assistance: "He gave the same rope, the same opportunity to all. He was not jealous of anything or anybody. But if it was his own ball game, he wanted the baseball and the bat and the glove. If you wanted to do it your way, he'd finance it, he'd help you do anything in God's green earth." One who was assisted by him commented: "It was almost like Mr. Warren was anxious to turn them loose, once he helped people."

Here as elsewhere his decisions were based on astute business insights. What is so commonly viewed as charity and sympathetic treatment also was an incapacity to do otherwise. He did not know how to be helpful, to afford opportunity, and at the same time to tie things together. There were a lot of strong young people coming up all around him, each wanting, as one of them put it, "his own chinaberry tree, his own rabbit ranch."

Warren Sewell was not an administrator; he did not know organization, nor did he know how to delegate. In his own firm he did not have people reporting to people. Rather he frequently had them fighting together for position. He did not possess the expert skill or vision to create an organizational umbrella that would afford expanding opportunity for rising young men in related clothing ventures. Nor did he seek that legal and organizational skill in others that could do it for him.

A Bremen resident spoke about this point, explaining that Warren Sewell was a salesman who became a manufacturer. He had someone else handle the manufacturing, someone else handle the numbers. "In his jump from the cotton row to manufacturing he remained an enthusiastic and great salesman, but he didn't match that in organizational ability or in entrepreneurial vision. He built what he did, and in the building of it he assisted the start of a lot of other related clothing things. But he didn't have to turn them loose or let them spin off. He simply didn't have the cast of mind to conceive of handling it or the ability to accomplish it."

Inevitably, some of the spin-off firms that Warren Sewell founded or assisted changed their nature or business structure and went into some line of the clothing business that competed with the Warren Sewell Clothing Company. Though these developments were distressing to his salesmen, Warren Sewell himself remained reasonably unconcerned. His record as a venture capitalist is impressive, and the list of firms and people he assisted in getting started is lengthy.

Sam Hubbard was the top salesman for the Stanley Pants Company of Chicago, and he and Warren Sewell met frequently on the road. Their conversations together and with Buncie Skinner, sales manager for a hat company, led them to agree to form a partnership to manufacture pants. At that time Sewell Manufacturing Company had pieces of cloth left over that could be made into pants.

The three agreed to meet in Bremen on a set day. But later Skinner felt he should not be involved and simply did not show. Hubbard then said he supposed that he had just as well go home, but Sewell said, "Naw, we'll get some other money 'round here." So he invited some of his staff and salesmen to put in shares, quickly raising the required amount.

Sewell and Hubbard each put in $18,000, and the hastily invited partners brought in another $14,000. This, then, was the start of Hubbard Pants Company with a beginning capitalization of $50,000.

For some of his staff who could not conveniently produce the approximately $2,000 required, Warren Sewell loaned it to them. When the company grew and prospered, Hubbard bought out all the others. One of the staff said the $2,000 he was told to borrow paid off handsomely. The firm became a nationally known producer.

Eventually the designer for Hubbard Pants, Otis Higgins, decided he wanted to have his own business, and in 1946 he told Hubbard he was going to resign and form his own company. When Hubbard phoned the news to Warren Sewell, who then owned more than fifty percent of Hubbard Pants, Sewell said, "That's fine, we'll all go in the pants business with Mr. Higgins." Neither wanted to lose him nor see him as a competitor. The two urged him to go into the pants business with them, with their putting up some of the money needed, which was done. Later Higgins wanted to go his own way and bought everyone else out.

Another individual who got his start with Warren Sewell was George Walls. His relationship with Warren Sewell brought him from bankruptcy into prosperity. He ran a shoe store in Cordele, Georgia, that failed.

He met Warren Sewell in Dallas, Texas, in 1934. He was working for a clothing consignment house that Sewell felt had real possibilities. He told Walls to go buy it, that he would furnish the money. Not until the purchase was completed did Walls learn that the money was intended as credit for him to buy the business himself. He turned to making the business a success and to paying off the loan he did not know he had taken.

Though he continued in business with Warren Sewell for years he never learned what his credit limit was. He never asked and was never told. Eventually Walls established his own business, a profitable and prosperous one specializing in workclothes and insulated-wear clothing.

Once Walls was looking for a place in Texas to move a store into and asked Warren Sewell to check it out for him. His report came back—the place has fine churches, nine schools, and no liquor stores—take it. He did, and the well located store grew to be successful.

In 1938 George Moses asked for and got a selling job with the Red Oak hat factory owned by Robert and Warren Sewell. Later he went on the road as a clothing salesman for Warren Sewell. After eight successful months of selling Warren told him in 1939 that he would set him up in a store in Louisiana, lending him $1,000 to get started. To the question, "Can you go?" Moses replied, "Not until tomorrow. I'm out of laundry."

Moses headed for Louisiana by train, with his laundry and his $1,000 and began forty-five years of business with Warren Sewell. He repaid the loan in 1940, but not until he sent his check the third time would Warren accept interest.

Moses did well with his store, formed his own company in Monroe, Louisiana, with Warren's assistance, and later branched out. He said he called Warren "steam shovel" because when he phoned him to order 50 suits, he always ended up with 150. Known in his home town as "Mr. Monroe," Moses each year remembers Warren Sewell by sending checks to two libraries in west Georgia.

They remained lifelong friends, frequently hunted to-gether—coon, mountain lion, and bear—and traveled com-panionably to Japan and India. He termed Warren Sewell "a benevolent Christian genius, a merchant prince in his indus-try," adding that Warren Sewell "got by getting, knew how to cast his bread upon the waters, and it usually came back."

Another person who prospered through Sewell's assis-tance was Earnest Marchman, the son of a Bremen druggist. Originally a shipping clerk for Roy Sewell's firm, Marchman was a salesman in Louisiana for Warren Sewell. The two es-tablished a firm in Louisiana, Monroe Manufacturing Com-pany, making Buccaneer slacks. At first Warren Sewell owned seventy-five percent of the company, then each owned fifty percent. At the end of World War II Warren Sewell arranged for his son-in-law, Jack Worley, son of an old-time company salesman, to become a partner in the Louisiana company with Marchman. The arrangement did not work out, and Worley returned to Bremen and to selling on the road.

When Ray Sewell, Warren's nephew, got ready to start in the pants business as a jobber, he had a talk with his Uncle Warren, who encouraged and advised him. "I didn't solicit any help from him, neither did I receive any." As his busi-ness grew he moved into manufacturing pants in several lo-cations. Eventually he had the usual young businessman's problem of securing capital for expansion.

Neither the local banks nor an Atlanta bank was suffi-ciently helpful, and Ray went to his Uncle Warren for advice on a banking source. He had never borrowed money from his uncle and did not go to borrow this time. He explained his circumstances and asked, "Uncle Warren, what would you do? How would you handle it?"

They went for a walk, discussed the matter, and came back to the house, whereupon, as Ray Sewell reported it: "Uncle Warren said, 'Here's the way I'd do it.' And he ran his hand down in his pocket and he come out with a check, just a plain old counter check from the Commercial Exchange Bank. He wrote Ray Sewell $250,000 and said, 'Don't you let your right hand know what your left is doing. You know what to do with that money, don't you?' "

Ray Sewell insisted on giving his uncle a note signed by himself and his wife and on paying interest. He then took the check and headed off to the bank and to his business. Among Ray Sewell's mementos is a photograph of his uncle's check and of his own, in final payment of the loan.

As noted previously in 1955 Lamar Plunkett, who had managed the Warren Sewell Company's Bowdon plant for ten years, decided to form a manufacturing company of his own. With the consent of his father-in-law, Warren Sewell, he formed LaMar Manufacturing Company of Bowdon, which made goods for the Warren Sewell Clothing Company and for others, especially Rothchild-Kaufman of Los Angeles, California. Through this business association there began a deep friendship among the Kaufmans, Alice and Irvin, and the Plunketts, the Sewells, and the entire clan.

Five years later in 1960, again with the consent of Warren Sewell, Plunkett formed a second firm, Bowdon Manufacturing Company, which purchased goods from his earlier-formed company and distributed them to retailers throughout the country.

Warren Sewell was cofounder for both these companies, his actual investment in each firm being two shares of common stock, one for himself and one for his wife. The two firms were successful from the start, remain so, and are important parts of the clothing manufacturing complex in west Georgia that was initiated by Warren Sewell.

Warren Sewell's role as entrepreneur was not limited to the clothing business but extended into agriculture. He was a poor farm boy in Graham before the turn of the century and retained a great love for the farmer. He knew the plight of the farmer—the lack of credit, the low payoff for agricultural products, the perishability of farm crops. The only thing he ever raised that was not perishable was cotton. All the rest—corn, peanuts, watermelons—were susceptible to loss unless brought to market quickly. As a farmer he sought something that would preserve his crops and get them to market quickly. In addition he desired a solution to the farmers' tough money problems.

In 1936 D. W. Brooks came to Carroll County, Georgia, seeking to form a farmers' cooperative. The idea was not well understood, especially by businessmen. Farmer cooperative movements were viewed by many as almost subversive and there were few Republicans who found the idea at all palatable. But in Carroll County Brooks found Warren Sewell—a farmer, a businessman, and a Republican—and told him of his hopes for a cooperative organization of farmers to help farmers. "You know," responded Warren Sewell, "I plowed with a mule until I was a grown man, and if there is anything I can do that will help raise the income of farmers I am for it, and I want to help." He became one of the directors of the Cotton Producers Association (later Gold Kist), was elected vice president at the first meeting and later chosen as president, a position he held until his death.

In the early days the association could not borrow enough money to carry on its work. Several times Warren Sewell signed notes to help raise the money. Once when the need was desperate, he put up $10,000 in cash. The association was constantly going to banks for help—New York, Chicago, the cooperative bank in Columbia, South Carolina. He was asked frequently to make these trips, for he was a banker himself, and his square-featured businessman's face and manner assisted an organization believed by many to be too liberal, too nonbusiness. He never refused a requested trip, though often the trips were emergencies and conflicted with his own buying trips. He always went, saying the farmers needed more help than he did.

The founder of the Cotton Producers Association, D. W. Brooks, pointed out that the association simply did not have enough collateral to carry on the kind of operation they had underway, and the banks were continually tightening the screws on them. "I always asked Mr. Sewell to go with me

Warren Sewell and D. W. Brooks, Cotton Producers Association meeting, 1963.

when I had one of these crises to see if we could straighten it out, and he always did."

The association became Gold Kist, a worldwide agricultural cooperative for production and marketing. One of the top farm cooperatives in the country, it is on the Fortune 500 list.

Warren Sewell was a banker, a venture capitalist, and a farmer. Born on a farm and having lived there until manhood, he loved farming and farm life. When at age sixteen he stood in the furrow and vowed a different kind of life for himself, he never considered that his determination would sever him from the soil on which he stood. With the first unencumbered money he earned, he bought farm land and retained the parcel always. He was a farmer at heart and remained a practicing farmer until his death. The hopes and aims of farmers, their economic plight, their crops, their beliefs—all these he kept close to him. "The stamp of the farm was placed on this fellow," said a Bremen businessman.

Warren Sewell registering for 1965 meeting, Cotton Producers Association.

This affinity for and attachment to the farm was not only sentiment but practicality. He lived through more than one business depression. The son of one of his close advisers said, "He kept the Graham farm so that if the sky fell in he could go back and live and eat. He raised cattle and had a big vegetable garden."

He attentively operated and looked after the home and farm at Graham owned by his father, then his mother, then his handicapped brother Byrd. By his own purchase he added acreage to it, managing and keeping up all of it as if it were his own. In so doing he provided an operating farm and home for his mother and Byrd.

In his lifetime he bought and sold a large amount of farm land elsewhere, not with real estate or developmental aims, but generally with the intent to operate a farm. On one occasion he did raise the bid a little on a block of land being auctioned off near Bremen and got the whole thing. He put this land in the company's family foundation and had

Warren Sewell's beloved home place, Graham, Alabama.

Raymond Otwell chop it up and sell it to various people. But essentially he bought land for his own farming wishes.

Once as he drove through south Georgia he stopped to observe a farm land auction underway, checked on a price he thought quite low, bid and bought the farm sight-unseen.

In brief he lived on and managed or supported the Graham farm. Too, he purchased and operated a large farm at Dawson in south Georgia and another in Terrell County for his brother. Then he bought two farms close to his home— the Lovvorn farm and a second one that he termed "the Rabbit Farm."

In south Georgia he owned a substantial farm in Terrell County plus pieces of farm acreage in two or three bordering counties. The Lovvorn and Rabbit farms and attendant acreage were in Carroll and Haralson counties, with Randolph County in Alabama containing all the Graham acreage.

The 1,200-acre south Georgia farm was two miles from Dawson and twenty-five miles from Albany. It had about thirty black tenant families living on it, a home for the farm manager, a farmhouse of sorts where Warren Sewell stayed when he was there, numerous barns and farm buildings, a smokehouse, and a cane mill. His farm manager operated a small store, where the workers could purchase overalls, shoes, and farm implements.

Richard Daniel, a black farm worker who grew up on the Graham farm with Warren, said he "was living pretty well" on the Dawson farm, as he was paid $2.50 a week and furnished housing, food, and clothing. When Warren Sewell was visiting there, explained Daniel, just at daylight he would "hear the hogs cutting up" and knew Warren Sewell was walking around the barns, dressed in overalls, leather boots, and a combat hat, ready for work. "I never saw any man who ever came close to him working," said Daniel. "He wouldn't axe a man to do anything he wouldn't do. He was a worker."

The farm produced pecans and an array of normal farm crops. Warren went to Texas to obtain big boar hogs for this farm and bred them locally all around south Georgia, to bring up the level of farm stock. He concentrated on raising prize Poland Chinas. For example, in September 1939 Warren Sewell, A. R. Lovvorn of Bremen, and Joe Martin of Carrollton sponsored a Dawson farm sale of fifteen bred sows, fifteen spring gilts, and twenty spring boars. There was also one herd boar, "The Tonic," out of Searchlight and McKenna's Marietta, with great bloodlines and all the fine characteristics of his famous sire, including "legs that are straight."

There are numbers of Sewell family anecdotes about one of the farm's prize acquisitions, a mid-west sow named Lady Guinivere. Warren's wife Ava grew a little tired of all the wires and telephone calls about the famous lady and her transportation and care and said, "After all, Lady Guinivere is just a pig."

Not all the farm pigs were prize. One of Warren Sewell's farm pleasures was assisting Richard Daniel to load pigs and drive them to one of the nearby market towns to sell.

The Internal Revenue Service interviewed Warren Sewell once, contending that the Dawson farm was not a true farming operation, but a hobby. "Hobby, hell," he responded, "you don't lose that much money on a hobby."

When the Dawson farm was sold, Bremen banker J. J. Mangham went down to observe the auction, taking his nineteen-year-old son, who marveled at the size of the crowd and of the barbecue: There were "fifteen pigs weighed about 200 to 300 pounds apiece on the barbecue pit. I never saw as much barbecue as he had down there, nor as much farm gear, tractors and plows, and so on. Everybody in that county must have bought a plow."

However, not all the farm equipment was sold, for Richard Daniel carried some of it up to the Graham farm; and he moved himself up also, into a Bremen house supplied by Warren Sewell. Daniel continued to work for him until he retired, having the right to occupy the house all his life.

In Terrell County Warren Sewell set up his brother Gay, who was ill, on a farm, hoping its operation and country life

Fixing the barbecue.

would assist his recovery. It did not, and in 1945 he had the Johnson Land Company auction the farm off. A young farmer from Carroll County with a family and several children bid the whole thing, intending to raise the purchase money by selling his Carroll County farm. On looking at the Carroll County farm and its indebtedness, Sewell felt that the young farmer was getting in over his head and that taking on the bigger farm would finally bankrupt him. He persuaded the young man to back out, and a couple of months later sold the Terrell County farm a second time, for much less than the first figure.

About 1947 or 1948 he bought the Lovvorn farm, three miles south of Bremen, from A. R. Lovvorn of the Warren Sewell Clothing plant. Sewell kept Black Angus cattle here. Cole Bell of the clothing plant went to this farm occasionally with him, both working at cutting silage or ditching with tractors. He gave Bell a black bull, getting him started with cattle on his own farm.

On the Rabbit Farm, which was supervised by a Mr. Durr who came with him from south Georgia, he raised cattle and kept saddle horses.

The Graham farm, about ten miles west of Bowdon in Randolph County, Alabama, was Warren Sewell's home, where his parents lived. Soon after Warren Sewell moved his business from Atlanta to Bremen, his father Willis died. Warren took over active supervision and support of his mother's farm and continued this oversight for many years.

A neighboring farmer said Warren Sewell made money in the clothing business "and happily spent or lost a portion of it on the Graham farm." At first he grew mostly cotton. There were black tenants on the place, and in the fall after the cotton went to gin and market, their year's accounts with Warren Sewell were settled up.

Warren's nephew Ray Sewell spoke of riding down with the mailman to visit his Grandmother Sewell's place when he was only "a little bitty knocker seven or eight years old." While there he would chop or pick cotton or bend corn. He recalled his Uncle Warren being busy at buying fertilizer for the farm and buying and trading mules—of which there were sixteen to twenty in the mule lots, for the use of all the tenant farmers on the place.

When cotton played out as a money crop, Sewell shifted to cattle. He grew grain and hay and constructed trench silos. The corn was cut, hauled up, ground, and stored in the trench silos until needed. In another approach to feeding he cut and shocked the corn in the field, later hauling the shocks to the pasture, where stalks and all were fed to the cattle. And finally he got tractors and a corn picker and put a hammer mill in one of the barns. He would grind the corn and feed the cattle right there.

He had a cane mill across from the farm house, where he ground both sorghum and ribbon cane and boiled down the juice into syrup. The fresh cane juice he drank by the dipperful, saying he never got enough. Perhaps he acquiesced in the children's requests for just one more swallow of juice, knowing its effect was like a strong spring tonic.

He once built broiler houses and raised chickens for the market, as did most of his Graham neighbors.

Filling an economical trench silo, 1920-1930.

A black family named Stephens worked in Graham for the Sewells for years, the mother cooking and baking, the boys Jimmie and Henry working in the fields and occasionally doing odd jobs around the plant. Jimmie worked for Warren Sewell twelve years, found him "all right to work for. Many a day he'd get out there and work with me in those bottom lands. Mr. Sewell wanted you to work, no standing around. I saw him all my life and had no complaints about him."

Roy Davis recounted a typical happy day at the farm with Warren Sewell, who picked him up and drove out there in the early morning. Sewell put on his overalls, and they spent the day repairing pumps and broken farm machinery, then grinding feed for the cows. They inspected Byrd's vegetable garden, sampled the spring onions freshly pulled, and ate a hearty country dinner, including "old time vegetables cooked in a black pot."

Similarly, Cole Bell told of riding from the plant with Warren Sewell "down to the old home place. He carried me back into his bottom land. He had some of the finest bottoms down in there, grass about knee high." He did not cut the grass to hay and put it in the barn, but let the tall grass bed down so that the cattle in the winter had dead grass on top, green beneath.

These were the same bottoms of the newly bought and unimproved Alabama farm that back in 1898 ten-year-old Warren and his father began clearing of their dense undergrowth—the worst of farm labors in the pre-tractor days. Since those 1898 labors the Graham farm, close to Warren's heart, always provided for him a haven, a dependable escape, and for his family a refuge and strength.

Aerial view of the Sewell family farmhouse.

·CHAPTER VI·

The Family
and Social Man

In late 1919 when Roy left college in Auburn and joined his two older brothers in Atlanta, their sisters had already married and were gone from the home. Left in the old Graham farmhouse were their father and mother, ages fifty-four and fifty-two, and their two younger brothers—Gay, who was nineteen and would marry a neighbor's daughter in 1923, and Byrd, sixteen.

For the next ten years while Warren lived and worked in Atlanta, he kept in close touch with his parents, visiting the Graham home frequently and stopping off there in connection with business trips. His father had quit drumming when the older boys left home and now occupied himself on the farm. Every now and then he came to Atlanta to watch the pants jobbing or manufacturing work and to talk and reminisce with the workers there. Hoyt Broadwell remembered him as a huge man, "a great conversationalist."

Following the early 1930 establishment of their manufacturing plant in Bremen, Warren continued to reside in Atlanta, traveled and sold, and was frequently in west Georgia. Just about the time he moved his plant to Bremen his father died, at age sixty-three, leaving in the Graham home his widow Willie, age sixty-five, and their son Byrd, twenty-seven. Warren's mother was to live in the family home for twenty-two more years, until she died at age eighty-seven.

In Atlanta in 1930 the Warren Sewells lived at 1440 Emory Road, NE. At the time Ava was forty-two, Warren forty-one, Frances thirteen, Charlotte nine, and son Warren one.

The parents, Ava and Warren, had been thoroughly involved in the fellowship and work of the Baptist church in Woodstock from the first days of their marriage. When they moved to Atlanta they attended the nearby Druid Hills Baptist Church. The city church was fortunate to gain two fully committed, hard-working, tithing new members. Warren, a Woodstock deacon, who had helped build and finance a new church building there, was experienced in church matters. Ava was as much a church goer as he was, interested in the congregation and its activities, especially in the Woman's Missionary Union.

The Sewells enjoyed their new church, though not until 26 January 1919, some time after moving to Atlanta, did they transfer their membership from the Woodstock church.

The Sewell family attended church regularly, for they believed the Sabbath was to be observed. There was no question that the children were to attend Sunday school, church, and BYPU, the youth organization. "I've seen my father go to church when the weather was no telling what," recalled a daughter.

His family did not play cards on Sunday, not even Old Maid for the children, who were grown before they saw a movie on Sunday.

Sometimes as he drove his daughters to church, he used the opportunity to discuss the week's derelictions and the faults to which even well-behaved girls were susceptible. One of the daughters said that the ten-minute drive from home to church was "the longest ride in Christendom."

He eventually served on the Druid Hills board of deacons, was its chairman at one time, and served as president of the men's Bible class. He was an active participant in church activities and careful to attend the funerals of friends when he was in town. Sometimes widows did not have money for even funeral expenses. Regularly he asked the pastor to check on the circumstances of widows; and if they needed help he gave the pastor a check so he could provide what was needed. Always sympathetic to the needs of women and children, he did not manifest as much sympathy for the men.

He taught a Sunday school class of teenage boys and felt there was more to it than what happened on Sunday mornings. He planned things for them to do during the week, including trips to the farm to spend the night in an old house, running trot lines at night, and cooking over an open fire in the fireplace.

Transportation to the farm was in what he called "the old plug," his big Buick. According to one of his class, Pastor W. Ches Smith III of the Tifton First Baptist Church, the boys never thought of him as a wealthy man but as "Mr. Warren," a friend and teacher who loved them and liked to be with them.

A few years after the Sewells joined the Druid Hills congregation a new pastor, Louie D. Newton, arrived. A layman who was not a theological seminary graduate, Dr. Newton had attended Mercer University and worked as a newspaperman. He and the Sewells became great friends. Warren took his preacher fishing with him, frequently to Florida and once to Alaska, and supplied him generously with clothing—new suits at the turn of every season. Newton was editor of the *Christian Index*, and evangelist Bob Jones, offended at one of his columns, sued him for slander. Warren Sewell backed his pastor and assisted the chairman of the board of deacons, a lawyer, Lon Duckworth, in a successful defense.

*(Left to right) Seated: Warren Sewell,
Methodist Bishop Arthur Moore, Baptist Pastor Louie Newton.
Standing: John Sibley, Ches Smith,
Presbyterian Pastor Wallace Alston, Culley Cobb.*

Many years after they met, when the pastor's retirement approached, Warren gave him a Cadillac, funded his retirement income, and helped the Druid Hills church buy Dr. Newton a home at 1011 Oakdale Road. After Dr. Newton retired in 1968 Warren Sewell moved his church membership from Druid Hills to the Bowdon Baptist Church.

On the theory that a man did not succeed in business through his own merits alone, he believed in sharing his prosperity. He had tithed in his early church years, and in Atlanta Dr. Newton persuaded him to continue. Warren Sewell was faithful in this activity and generous almost to a fault in assistance beyond his tithe. Over and over he would say that a man should never die with any of the Lord's money in his pocket. He simply could not give enough, was asked for much, and responded readily.

Several of his finest salesmen and staff came from the congregation. He always kept his eye open for promising men. Young Warnock, whose father—the owner of a general store—bought pants from Warren the drummer, rented an apartment from them in 1918 just before going off to World War I. In 1935 Sewell recruited him to be Pastor Newton's administrative assistant, a position he held for forty-three years. After Warnock's son graduated from Georgia Tech following World War II, Warren Sewell hired him in 1946 for a job in the clothing plant.

In a somewhat similar fashion Warren Sewell employed another congregation member, J. Mac Smith, who was the son of Ches Smith, Jr., a fellow church member and fishing companion of Warren. In the church parking lot one Sunday Warren stopped young Smith, who had just graduated from Mercer University, asking him to consider coming to Bremen to work in the clothing business.

Both Ava and Warren read the Bible daily. At breakfast their beloved black cook and maid Josie read aloud from the scriptures with them. When he grew older and reading was more difficult, his black driver, Clyde (Buck) Newell, came to the house for breakfast and read the Bible to him. He always believed in reading the scriptures aloud at festivals and meals

J. Mac Smith   Parks Warnock, Jr.

during the Thanksgiving and Christmas seasons. When he was hospitalized, the nurse read to him from the Bible every day.

Said a daughter: "I never sat down to a meal with him that he didn't say grace." He believed in prayer and was on his knees every night before he slept. He was childlike and unabashed about praying. Hunting in the wilds of New Mexico in cold weather he knelt under the open sky on his sleeping bag and prayed, then crawled in to warmth and sleep.

Explained a daughter about his prayers: "He didn't say 'bless the children' but he'd say 'Lord, we are so thankful for Charlotte and Frances. We are so thankful for Warren' or if the grandchildren were present, he named them, one by one."

As one devoted to country church singings, he sang in church, happily and with volume and resonance. Once when an embarrassed granddaughter whispered to her mother that he was singing too loudly, Charlotte replied: "Hush, honey, Daddy's happy."

He urged his workers to support their church, to attend church regularly. Many of his staff he taught to tithe. Any preacher, of any faith or color, who visited his plant got a free suit of clothes.

Warren Sewell and his machinery maintenance men both suffered because of the no-Sunday-work rule. He really meant it, but he also wanted the plant to roll on Monday morning. If in order to have the operators at work on Monday, the maintenance crew was changing or repairing the machines on a Sunday, invariably Warren Sewell appeared, saying, "You know I don't approve of this. Why are you working on Sunday?"

Once the pressing room gang came in on Sunday afternoon to shift machinery around, and Warren Sewell appeared, asking: "Did the ox get in the ditch on Sunday?" The foreman recalls that his boss was not satisfied with the explanation and the crew never did it again.

These no-Sunday-work occurrences reveal in some measure how his life was governed by a balance of work and religion. He also sought a balance of work and family.

One of his daughters explained how he weighed the important aspects of his life: "You can't review Daddy's life and leave out God. Daddy's first love in life was God. Momma used to say the second one was business. I don't know if business or family came second."

To some degree Warren Sewell was harder on his family than he was on others, certainly harder to get access to, or to secure a sympathetic hearing from. An innately gracious man, he was ready to listen to the countryman seeking two thousand dollars, but not so ready to afford a family member an equally open and ready hearing. In business concerning the plant he felt more comfortable—more able to be open and direct—with those who were not directly related to him.

An employee testified: "He always looked after all the family, but in dealing here in the plant he'd rather deal outside his family. But he looked after them and loved them. I don't know if the grandchildren know how to appreciate what they've got or not. He always said, 'Three generations, from shirtsleeves to shirtsleeves.' We'll see." Said a stockroom employee: "He had more patience with me than he had with his own son or his sons-in-law."

When Warren Sewell's son Warren was born in 1929, he and his wife were forty-three and forty-two. He was born late in their lives. Then, as always, Warren Sewell was much occupied with his struggling business and, except for weekends, away from home. As it had been for the daughters, the care and upbringing of the son fell to the mother.

Had Warren Sewell been a man interested in sports, he might well have been involved with his children in them. But with no real hobby except perhaps fishing, these contacts were limited.

Sewell could be understanding about growing boys when he had time for it. In the early 1940s when Warren and his cousin Roy were playing ball in the plant parking lot, one of them hit a ball directly into Warren Sewell's office window, smashing it. He came outside and mildly said, "Boys, you're going to have to play baseball somewhere else."

There was no question that he loved and cared for his children, all of them, and all of his extended family. He tried to show it to them by providing for them, then and in the future. His push to get his business going was so great, his commitment of time to it so large, that some aspects of the father-child relationship suffered.

Warren Sewell believed in every child doing some type of useful work. In Atlanta Charlotte worked during the Easter and Christmas seasons in one of the downtown Sewell clothing stores. But she always had a problem with embarrassment when male customers asked her about selecting and purchasing their underwear.

Young Warren raised chickens in the backyard at the Springdale home—feeding, watering, collecting the eggs. He went from door to door in the neighborhood, selling pecans grown on the south Georgia farm.

In October 1939 at a dinner party next door to the Springdale home the Sewells' daughter Frances, twenty-two, met a dinner guest, Lamar Plunkett, twenty-eight. They were married a year later in October 1940.

In August 1941 the Sewells' second daughter, Charlotte, twenty, married Jack Worley, twenty-four, the son of an old-line Sewell Clothing Company salesman.

Both the Sewell daughters and their husbands were caught up in the war. Son Warren was at home attending high school. Frances was away at West Point, New York, with her Army husband, Lamar Plunkett. Charlotte's Air Force husband was overseas, serving with the Troop Carrier Command and as personal pilot to General Mark Clark. To the delight of her parents, Charlotte, married just nine months, lived with them for three years while working for Eastern airlines and awaiting her husband's return.

Warren Sewell was constantly on the road selling, but also seeking woolen and other cloth that was scarce during the war years. When he was in town, he would meet the late-

Marriage of Charlotte Sewell and Jack Worley, August 1941.

afternoon streetcar at The Byway, so his daughter did not have to walk home in the dark; and in the mornings he would drive her to the trolley stop, waiting with her until it arrived. When he was gone, she walked to and from the trolley or, if there was gasoline, drove her own car.

After work Charlotte did volunteer Pink Lady work from 7 to 10:30 in the evening at Emory Hospital, two blocks away. In other activities she and her mother attended movies together, went to concerts, and saw Warren Sewell on the weekends.

The war years sped by quickly. With the end of the war and the split of the Sewell brothers' clothing business, the husbands of both daughters went into the family clothing business. All of them became caught up in the hard work and excitement of developing a new company from scratch.

When Warren and Ava's son Warren graduated from the University of Georgia in June 1950, he went to work full-time with the Warren Sewell Clothing Company. In June 1952 Warren, who was twenty-three years old, married Mary Virginia Thomas, twenty-one, also a University of Georgia graduate.

Warren Sewell always helped his family. Whatever his priorities were, in a quiet, unobtrusive way he demonstrated a love and support for his family, all his family. Without any thought of reward or return he provided food, payment of doctor bills, homes, jobs, house repairs, housing, nursing-home care, hospitalization, education expenses, advice, and business guidance.

In speaking of Warren Sewell balancing work and business, a clothing mill salesman from out of state said: "He did those things, and a lot of other things, with grace and openness and agreeability."

He had a large family with a lot of problems. A Bremen merchant said: "I never saw Mr. Warren Sewell that he didn't respect and love his relations, whether he agreed with them or not. He took care of and suffered with his family and never gave up on them." The son of one of his close advisers said: "When you consider the problems his family inflicted on him, you wonder. But the care he gave was infectious; it impacted on all of us in the plant, on all our families, and on the community."

Warren Sewell once laughingly said, without reference to anyone or any occurrence: "You know, you can choose your friends, your kinfolks are thrust upon you." Sometimes one thinks he might have had his relatives in mind when he said that he daily prayed for patience.

He had an intense and deep commitment to help all his family, not just his mother and father. This was an absolute commitment to doing well for everyone, which appears almost a saintly characteristic. But it has another side to it: the zeal for doing well for everyone meant that sometimes decisions were made for others. Yet these other people needed, for their own life and development, to be making these decisions themselves. This zeal put a burden on others that Warren Sewell did not understand. It hampered both his business and his family relations.

An aspect of Warren Sewell's family life that stands out was his attachment to his mother—Will Roop said he was the finest mother's boy in the world—and to his handicapped brother, Byrd. Said a plant employee and neighbor: "He had a wonderful relationship with his mother and with his handicapped brother, Byrd, who stayed with her. He went to see them many times when he did not have the time. If she wanted anything, he saw that she got it."

When his father died and his mother inherited the Graham house and farm, Warren promised her he would always keep the farm as a home for Byrd. And he did. For more than two decades his mother and brother shared the house, then Byrd lived in it alone until his death.

Keeping the farm meant maintaining it also, and various of the plant employees, especially maintenance workers, were over the years frequently at the farm, fixing pumps, doing renovation, repairing roofs. After Willie Sewell's death farmer-friends continued to spend part of the weekends on Byrd's Graham farm, being helpful.

Warren Sewell amid family group, 1951.
Left to right, standing: Lou Darnell, Guy Darnell, Lamar Plunkett,
Warren Sewell, Jr., Mary Sewell.
Seated: Charlotte Worley holding Carol Worley, Ella Fowler, Warren Sewell,
Ava Sewell, Frances Plunkett.
Children seated: Thomas Plunkett, Richard Plunkett, Guy Darnell, Jr.

His secretary put it exactly: "He kept the farm as a place for Byrd to be free." And he was free and safe, or as Robert Tisinger put it, "happy as he could be till he died."

Safe on the farm, he ran and walked, uninhibited and free. Not able to handle a car, he drove a spanking buggy and a splendid but durable and easy-to-handle Morgan horse, both provided by Warren.

Once when Byrd's buggy had been well used for years, Warren decided to surprise him with a new one. It was a special order from far away and was assembled in the plant under Warren's constant and careful supervision. When it was ready and presented to Byrd, he just got in and drove busily off, unimpressed as to whether his buggy was old or new. But as a townsman who witnessed the event said, the new buggy was very important to Warren, who delighted in it and commented on it at every turn.

Byrd knew everyone in the surrounding countryside and like his father was a great one to set out in the buggy in order to socialize.

He was a real Sewell, always in a hurry. Once Byrd arrived unexpectedly at Mrs. Saxon's mother's house in his buggy. He put the horse in the barn and came in the house, saying: "Ellen, hurry up, I've got to eat my lunch and go. I have lots of things to do."

John Cook, manager of the Bremen-Bowdon Investment Company, can show one the metal hitching ring, deeply embedded in a large oak outside the office, where Byrd tied his horse when he visited the plant.

Byrd perhaps had more friends than any other Sewell family member. He was enormously popular. Said one of his numerous female cousins: "Everybody, cousins and all, would have fought for Byrd."

He loved to sing and frequently drove to church singings, where he triumphantly joined in, holding the book upside down, for he could not read.

Byrd loved growing things and was a splendid gardener. He planted tomatoes and onions and always grew turnip greens, which he supplied to a number of plant employees on a regular basis. Warren Sewell was fond of garden vegetables. No visit to the farm was complete without a look at the garden, especially the onions, which he and Byrd pulled up by the handfuls, with Byrd saying: "Uncle Warren, these sure are good."

Said a close family friend of Warren: "His devotion to his mother and his brother Byrd radiated to others less close than family." The persistent help he gave to his mother and Byrd was matched by assistance to his other brothers and to his sisters.

Warren Sewell's business relations with his brothers Robert and Roy have been traced, and to some extent his personal relations also. Beginning in the early Graham farm days as the oldest and his mother's right arm, Warren shouldered responsibilities and provided leadership. This family role could not always have been comfortable.

He assisted Robert and Roy with their schooling, helped them to get established in Atlanta, joined with them in business, and took in Roy, who had no capital, as a partner. When Robert's hat business foundered, he bought it, sold it back as desired by Robert, then bought it back again. He purchased Robert's share of the Sewell Clothing Company when Robert wished to sell. When Robert, ill and despondent, took his life in 1939, he assisted his widow, who attempted to run the hat business. When it failed, he gave her help all her life.

Regarding the early Graham days, Roy testified that Warren was both father and older brother to him. In his later life Roy explained that he was "a gay and handsome dog and Warren looked after me." He termed Warren the most unselfish man he ever knew and worried always because he would not keep his shoes shined.

Warren came to an accommodation with Roy when his younger brother chafed under his management of the Sewell Manufacturing Company, selling it all to him. They became good competitors and remained as close as brothers could be. Once after they went their individual ways in business Roy, concerned that Warren was selling suits more cheaply than he was, spoke to Warren, who gave him no direct response. Roy exploded: "Warren, you are the damn best brother in the world—but you are also the damnest brother!"

For his brother Gay, ill much of his life, he proffered a farm and farm life in Terrell County, employment in the clothing plant, and operation of a clothing store in Atlanta.

His sisters were sent to college, and after marriage when they needed help, he gave it. His widowed sister, Lois Whitehead, he brought from Birmingham, established her in a home near Graham, and gave her employment in the plant as well as the lunchroom concession.

Warren and his younger brother Roy.

For both Lois and his sister Lura Teague he dispatched plant maintenance workers to keep their homes in repair. Said a plant electrician: "Mr. Sewell said, 'Now I want you to take care of my sisters, whatever they need.' When they had anything to do down there, I went right away."

When a cousin lost her last brother, Warren approached her, saying he would be her brother. "I thought no," she said, "but in a week I was calling him. He told me what to do, expected me to do it without foolishness or wavering. And I did. He has always been like a brother to me." He also assisted nieces in attending college and securing professional schooling.

With his children he attempted an evenhandedness that may not at all times have been so perceived, but was meant to be. When his wife Ava died, he had all her best jewelry appraised, divided into three equal parcels, and boxed. The three children drew lots in order of age. He took the same balanced approach on money, bonds, stocks for the children. "He was," said one of them, "very careful to be fair."

His driver Clyde (Buck) Newell said, "He always made time for his children." When asked late in his life about his philosophy on children and grandchildren, he responded that they were the greatest thing in the world, "but on the other hand they must be prepared for life. Give them a college education if you can, but be sure to teach them how to work, that is the main thing."

To both sons-in-law he granted opportunity for work experience and future affluence in the plant.

His wife Ava died suddenly of a heart attack on 15 November 1958; she was seventy years old and they had been married forty-six years. Their marriage had been a good one. When Warren Sewell wept at her loss, it was the only time his children ever saw him cry.

The family was afraid for him to stay alone, so his young grandson Tom moved in with him. Josie, the maid and cook, and Tom cared for him and afforded him company. He and Tom went for a walk each day, after school for one and work for the other, and had long and animated conversations.

Tom slept in the next room on a day bed to be close, and was occasionally kept awake by the high volume of his deaf grandfather's radio or by his talking while asleep.

At seventy the widower Warren Sewell was personable, well known, vigorous, wealthy. As time went on after his wife's death it became clear that a number of ladies—of his own age and some younger—were interested in him and in marriage. He kept his peace, his own counsel, and finally quietly let it be known that he was marrying an Atlanta widow of his own age, Ina Tuggle Morgan.

A saying attributed to him at this time was that he would rather smell an old lady's liniment than a young girl's perfume—a remark that, if true, must have miffed some young women and amused his new wife.

It was an ideal second marriage for both. The families had lived close to each other in Atlanta—the Warren Sewells at 1102 Springdale Road, the Morgans close by on Briarcliff. Members of the two families were good friends, attending the same church and sitting together in the same pew each Sunday. The men were in the same Sunday school class, as were Ava and Ina. The families vacationed and traveled together. Ina's husband had operated a successful jewelry store on Alabama Street, and on his death Warren served as his executor.

The families had been close enough for the couple to know much of each other. Ina could see Warren's long suits and any shortcomings, and he knew her. She was a quiet sort of person, as he was. She knew what to expect of marriage to him, what her life would be like. She did not need marriage for the sake of money or support. She was comfortably well off. A prenuptial agreement cared for Ina in the event of his death. It also made provisions for two families and preserved to each their estate.

There were four daughters in the Morgan family, near the ages of Frances and Charlotte. Ina's big and close family was good for Warren Sewell. He gained a new family at a time in his life when he had the time and inclination to enjoy it. He appreciated this family life and his stepdaughters felt themselves lucky to have two such splendid fathers.

After ten years of marriage the Warren Sewells moved from Atlanta to Fairview Avenue in Bremen. Their daughter Charlotte and her husband Jack Worley lived in the house next door to them for a decade.

The Sewells also had a house in Bowdon, eighteen miles away and close to the plant. They spent time in each place. When asked where she lived, Ina replied: "Six months in Bremen, six months in Bowdon; six months in Bremen, six months in Bowdon." To the question, "Did you get tired of this?" her laughing response was, "I didn't say so."

Warren Sewell homes, Bremen and Bowdon.

"Six months in Bremen, six months in Bowdon."

Warren Sewell always got restless in the Bremen house, because at the other home he had a small fishing pond and a garden, in which he even had a peanut patch. The summers were always busy, for there was the Bowdon garden along with the harvesting, preserving, and canning that recurred each year.

One of the neighbors marveled at the pains he took with his bean stakes, carefully putting them under cover at the end of the season until the next year.

In 1930 the Warren Sewells brought into the household a young black girl of sixteen from the Graham farm, Josie Stephens. Her initial chore was to watch after Warren, who was four years old and very active. Ava taught Josie to iron, to cook, and generally to run the household, which she did capably and with devotion. All grew to love her.

When Warren Sewell's diabetes required special treatment, Josie was of substantive help in seeing that he usually adhered to his diet. Not only did she become a great cook but a resilient one, reacting to the arrival of sudden guests at odd hours with calm efficiency.

Scores of visitors in the home were impressed by her wit and insight and by the completely natural fashion in which she was in and of the Sewell family.

Warren Sewell built Josie a four-room brick apartment over the garage in the rear of their home, and she lived there as a part of the family. After she married and had children—two boys, Bobby and Jean, two years apart—she would bring the babies into the Sewell kitchen each morning, keeping them in a basket under the table. The Sewells couldn't help but spoil these children.

Charlotte, recalling Josie's children in the Sewell kitchen, said that she herself cleaned as many little black fannies as white. When Josie's boys grew older, they lived on the Graham farm with Josie's mother.

Warren Sewell arranged that Josie be provided with a home for her lifetime, so after his death Frances and Lamar

*Standing: Maid and cook Josie Stephens
with Frances Plunkett and (seated) Warren Sewell.*

Plunkett moved her to a house near them and cared for her. She died in 1981, age seventy-five and mourned by many.

Warren Sewell enjoyed life. Said the wife of one of his closest advisers, "He loved everybody, and you know with all his hard work he had a lot of fun. Not so many people can have all the problems he had and relish life too."

He enjoyed himself and was attracted to simple pleasures, interesting stories, visiting friends, good food. He took time for this enjoyment. He liked being with people, and after his wife Ava died he continued to have eight or ten of his church friends by the Springdale home for dinner and spirited conversation.

One of the sustaining forces in his life was his optimism. He retained a cheerful, outgoing nature in the face of difficulties that would have swamped a lesser man. "Warren Sewell was cheerful, serene in his faith, and trusted his own judgment and abilities," said one of his advisers. A Bremen businessman stated that he "always found him on the bright side of everything. He was a good man to have around. I never heard him say a harm word about anybody." His pastor termed him "a graduate of the university of life summa cum laude."

Warren Sewell had a great sense of love and feeling for little country churches in the area where he grew up, places like Shiloh and Camp Ground. These churches had all-day to-dos, when the ladies of the congregation spread lunch on the grounds, and he attended many of these, frequently in company with his nephew Ray Sewell. They were often joined by his brother Byrd, driving his buggy.

Warren Sewell relished the simple enjoyment of church singings and attended them frequently, as well as singing conventions at places like Indian Creek, the camp ground at Shiloh, Graham, and up at Kansas. He contributed to the publication of Sacred Harp hymnals and found simple and full enjoyment in joining in vigorous song, tapping his foot, and raising and lowering his arm with the rhythm as the crowd praised the Lord in four-part harmony. His wife Ava was a music major at Tift College, played the piano beautifully, and loved music—but not all-day singings, which she considered too countrified. Warren, though, never stopped relishing group singing, with the vibrations bouncing off the wooden church walls.

Almost all who knew Warren Sewell say that he had no hobby, or that people or work or making money was his hobby. A constant comment on the subject is that for him it "mostly was work and then his family."

He was truly a worker and devoted himself to operating a successful business. His deep absorption in his work left room for little else, or so it appeared. Perhaps it left nothing of sufficient size or importance to be classified as an avocation or a hobby.

Nonetheless the list of his areas of interest and concern outside his clothing business and family covered a remarkable range. There was farming, in particular the Graham farm where his parents lived and where his mother resided for

North Georgia singing group with their portable organ,
Corinth Baptist Church, Resaca, Georgia, early 1900s.

years after his father's death. He gloried in the church and its
work. He loved banking and was wrapped up all his life in
it, its problems and joys and benefits.

Among his other activities were fishing, hunting, horses,
and horse shows. And he was agreeable to and willingly
supported his wife Ava's deep interest in antiques.

He relished fishing, especially in company with others—his son, his sons-in-law, his pastor, plant employees,
friends. For many years he organized semi-annual fishing
jaunts to Panacea, Florida, for and with the stockroom employees and with friends from Atlanta. They stayed at the
Tallahassee Yacht Club, operated by a retired Coast Guard
captain whose wife supervised meal preparation for the
parties.

Frequently he would meet Atlanta friends, such as Hugh
Altman and Ches Smith, his automobile dealer and fellow-
Baptist, at the Druid Hills Baptist Church. Here they listened
to Dr. Louie Newton's sermon, and as soon as it was over,
the group, including the pastor, drove to Panacea. It would

Warren Sewell, Jr., Banker J. J. Mangham, and Warren Sewell exhibiting the day's catch of fish, Guntersville, Alabama, June 1946.

not be dark when they arrived, but there was no Sunday fishing. Warren Sewell would not wet a line on Sunday, but they did play rook, canasta, and setback to pass the time—although not with any betting.

They would fish for a few days, during which he would make advance arrangements for two groups of plant employees coming later. The first group drove from west Georgia Sunday afternoon, fished Monday, Tuesday, and Wednesday until noon, then headed home. The second group left west Georgia Wednesday noon, meeting the returning group on the way to exchange news. The second party fished Thursday, Friday, and Saturday till noon.

The same guides and boats were provided to both groups, and Warren Sewell covered all the expenses. In addition to affording his workers recreation he took pains to mix in each group men from both the Bremen and Bowdon locations.

The fishing was good, the guides were excellent. They went out in small boats that carried two people and had two motors. Once out from shore they used one motor for trolling or for moving in along the piers to find red fish.

Their pleasures were simple. Before retiring they had a period of devotion, with Warren Sewell reading from the scriptures or perhaps Louie Newton, if he was there. Each evening this period was closed by a different member of the group saying a prayer.

On one trip the sole Methodist member of the group was thoughtful of his circumstances among the Baptists and Baptist Pastor Newton. While fishing he prepared himself by rehearsing his prayer. Sure enough, that evening he was called on to pray, and he performed ably, rendering a good Methodist devotion. That a benighted Methodist could perform this well so impressed Dr. Newton that as soon as the concluding "amen" came, the Baptist preacher burst out with a surprised: "Hallelujah, hasn't it been a good day?"

The fishermen shared rooms, and the employee who roomed with his boss found out, if he did not already know, that Warren Sewell knelt by his bed and prayed before retiring.

Bountiful good food, especially seafood, was one of the attractions of the vacation, particularly for Warren Sewell. One of the stockroom employees, whose appetite was on the light side, protested at the size and diversity of the food order Warren Sewell was putting in for him. The response was, "I'll go ahead and order it, and if you can't handle it, I'll do away with it for you."

Once when part of the group was driving back they stopped in Albany to change drivers, and Warren Sewell went in the store to get them some food—sardines, a large and strong bermuda onion, and an apple. On their way again, he opened the sardines, sliced the onion and apple, and passed around helpings. The driver, silently overwhelmed by the strength and aroma of the food combination, thought he could escape by saying he was driving and did not want any. His boss would spear a helping of each on his penknife blade and point it at him, saying, "Big man, gotta eat." The driver said it was a long ride home.

At his house in Bowdon Warren Sewell had a small fish pond, and he would permit stockroom employees to fish there when they wished. A time or two, when an employee seemed to him to be pretty well beaten down, he would send him to the pond during working hours.

He owned a single-shot bolt-action .22 rifle, a pistol, and a couple of shotguns, including a splendid double-barreled Parker. His farm tenants kept hunting dogs for him, especially on the south Georgia farm. He hunted birds and rabbits occasionally, and while on the south Georgia farm enjoyed coon hunting, tramping through the woods with the black farmhands, making a fire, and waiting for the dogs to tree. Louie Newton went coon hunting with him now and then, as did George Walls, a clothing merchant. Walls enjoyed the hunts, but complained that they always gave him the task of lugging the crosscut saw used to bring down the tree to which the coon had retreated. As Walls would carry the saw through the woods, it caught on vines and undergrowth.

Warren and Walls went to the New Mexico wilds once, escorted by Zane Grey's guide. There they hunted bear and mountain lion, traveled by horseback, and carried all their gear and food on pack animals. Walls was impressed that Sewell, a persistent buttermilk drinker, somehow managed to insert into their sparse gear one-gallon cartons of buttermilk in metal containers, secured from an El Paso dairy.

On the mountain hunting trip Warren Sewell drew a recalcitrant horse named Frank that persistently bucked him out of the saddle every morning. He said little about it, merely picking himself up and mounting again. But near the end of the trip, Walls observed him talking to the horse and asked about it. "Oh, I've just promised Frank a present when we get back—a sawed-off baseball bat over the head if he throws me again." Later in the day he remarked, "I really can't blame Frank, he's a spirited animal."

Sewell kept saddle horses on his farms and liked to ride. For years he and Ed Morris of the stockroom went to the walking-horse shows in Shelbyville, Tennessee. A customer there had a box seat and would invite Warren Sewell and Morris, who waited on the customer, up every year to observe the world series of the walking horses. The customer took them to see the barns and farms, and Warren Sewell delighted in the horses, the fellowship, and the good food. He returned year after year.

Once he went to the Kentucky Derby, spending the night as a guest at one of the big horse farms. His host asked him to bet on the farm's entry, and he risked two dollars. The race was an upset, and he won heavily. He was not a gambling man, so on the first Sunday back home he quietly put in the collection plate his winnings, a tight roll of bills with a rubber band around it.

Warren Sewell traveled much, saw a lot of the world, and expressed his belief that "the greatest education a person can have is by traveling." There were only two places in the world for him: first, his home area of Graham-Bremen-Bowdon, then all the rest of the world. He loved going out to compare, secure in the knowledge that home was the best place and would remain so. When he returned home from travels abroad, his feelings were akin to those of Martin Luther when he first saw Rome.

Ava, his first wife, did not travel much with him, remaining at home to keep house and be with the children. Eventually they traveled to Europe together, where she had a stroke, which shortened somewhat their travels.

They brought back gifts for their children and grandchildren and friends. One staff member received something he had always dreamed of owning—a Borsalino hat.

Sewell's European letters to his children, written in an easy-flowing, beautiful, almost copper-plate hand, were full of spirited comments about all he saw and contained almost none of the usual tourist complaints. Virtually every letter included suggestions and admonitions about his home church and its operation.

At every major city along his foreign travels he expected to have waiting for him the New York newspaper clippings sent by his secretary back home.

His traveling companions always relished his company, telling how on a brief stop in Alaska's capital he returned from what they thought was a typical tourist stroll to see the sights, only to learn that he had visited several stores and sold clothing orders. In India he dutifully left his shoes at the main entrance to a temple and strolled with the party. But when they came upon a snake charmer and a cobra, he deserted them, returning to their automobile outside and sending his driver back for his shoes.

On a Far Eastern trip he was eager to locate a Baptist church for his Sunday worship. In Tokyo after much difficulty in finding a Baptist church, he was downcast that the services were in Japanese. Concerned that the congregation might have noticed his disappointment, he quietly left $100 in the collection plate.

After his health declined somewhat his doctor asked him to curtail his flying, but Warren and Ina still made short trips. In 1962 they went to Europe for two months. On the return home they went to California for the Southern Baptist Convention, then he went to Alaska for a fishing trip. After this he went to Peru on a trip sponsored by Gold Kist.

One pleasure he had was in games, at home or with friends on fishing trips. He played Rook and setback and occasionally canasta with his wife Ava. Once in Atlanta while their children were still at home, there was a great sleet storm that kept them house-bound for three or four days. They had received for Christmas a newly introduced game, Monopoly. Warren, Ava, Frances, Charlotte, and Warren kept a running contest going for three days.

After Ava died in November he spent Christmas with his daughter Charlotte and her family—a restrained and somewhat sad holiday. After the grandchildren were in bed they completed the Santa Claus arrangements, then played setback until two in the morning.

*Travelers Warren and Ina Sewell
in Jerusalem.*

On board the Queen Elizabeth.

His wife Ava was interested in antiques before they were married and had a deep and well-developed understanding of them, especially of furniture. She became an avid collector. Warren hardly knew what an antique was, but he learned. He encouraged her in her collecting, assisted her, and occasionally bought for her. On their travels, both domestic and abroad, he dutifully visited antique shops with her. Now and then he surprised her by quietly ascertaining what she really wanted, not what she said she wanted, and buying it.

He enjoyed another of her hobbies, a beautiful flower garden, seeing in it a continuation of his mother's green thumb and love of country beauty. In the same fashion he almost daily visited his daughter Charlotte's orchid collection. For ten years they lived next door to each other, and the orchid collection, which he encouraged her to begin, was of daily interest to him.

Some hobbies of others were of little interest to him. One of these was golf. Warren Sewell and Sam Hubbard were good friends and somewhat alike. Once after attending a party in Savannah, Sam remarked to Warren that the folks there were really dumb, "not one of them knew anything about making pants."

Neither man played golf, and they manifested no interest when their colleagues played. Once their staffs decided to interest them in the game. They took up a collection, bought them clubs, and finally got them onto a course. The two played a few holes but mostly talked business and clothes; they quit before they completed the game. That was the end of the golf experiment.

When Ed Morris of the stockroom came down with a bleeding ulcer, Warren Sewell gave him Saturday afternoon off for recreation. Morris started playing golf, and each Monday his boss would ask him about his game. In time Warren Sewell became accommodated to the game and his staff playing it. Said one worker, "Ed Morris made golf respectable."

Warren Sewell was no athlete and had only a marginal interest in organized sports. However, he regularly bought tickets to all Georgia Tech football games and gave them to interested staff members.

Sewell was a good neighbor and a man deeply involved in his community in all kinds of ways. An important and powerful man, he never forgot the wellsprings of his life, his poor farm background, his common origin with his fellows. He had a pervading sense of fairness, of never taking advantage—a good salesman's instinctive aversion to unfounded profit of any sort. He once sold a farm in the Graham area at auction and later learned that the purchaser intended moving into his old house on the farm. Knowing the well there had no water, he quietly dispatched workers there to dig a well, saying, "That man's got to have some water down there."

He bid on a Bremen house being auctioned off, then learned one of his employees had also put in a bid and that it had been his boyhood home. He withdrew his bid and quietly assisted the man to purchase the home.

He was not particularly attuned to participating openly and actively in the political process. Sewell did not get involved in any public endorsement, nor did he seek office himself. He did not often become involved in the political activities or factions of town or county.

Though he voted for FDR in 1932, he was a staunch Republican and made campaign contributions now and then, some considerable in size, to state and national candidates. However, any zeal he had for making substantial contributions was tempered by the two loans he made to an Atlanta Republican candidate for governor, neither of which was repaid.

In other ways he participated personally and vigorously in fellowship and civic activities. Like all the Sewells he was a great believer in and supporter of the Masons. He belonged to the lodge in Graham, attending there and in Bremen frequently.

At age twenty-one he received all three Masonic degrees on Christmas Day, 1909, in Heaton Lodge 354 of Graham, Alabama. In 1912, the year of his marriage and establishment of his home in Woodstock, Cherokee County, Georgia, he shifted membership from Graham, joining Woodstock's Lodge 246 in September 1913. In 1941 he affiliated with Bremen Lodge 456 and remained a member until his death. He received his Grand Lodge Fifty-Year Award 21 December 1962.

He went to lodge meetings regularly and took great pride and pleasure in attending when family members or employees were raised in grade. He encouraged his son and his sons-in-law to be Shriners. His nephew Ray recalled his Uncle Warren's disappointment when he learned that Ray, plagued by lack of time and scheduling problems, had been raised without his being present.

When young men were employed and started on their apprenticeship in the stockroom, Warren Sewell spoke to them about the Masons, not urging, but informing and offering help. At one time, estimated a longtime salesman, eighty or ninety percent of the salesmen on the road, almost all graduates of the stockroom or other plant positions, were Masons.

He was firmly convinced of the worth of Masonic activity, both to the individual and to the community. In addition to attending and working in the lodge himself, he encouraged and assisted others to join, and gave generously to insure that lodges had appropriate meeting places.

Though a generous man, Warren Sewell never felt he had given enough. Perhaps he was always thinking of his story about the Lord's money and was constantly trying to insure that if he died, he would not have any of the Lord's money in his pocket. What the appropriate share was for charitable and compassionate causes he never decided. If asked for a good cause he gave, frequently right at that moment.

A lifelong friend said of him: "He made lots of money—knew how to make money, and how to use money to the glory of God—how to master money rather than letting money master him." Another old friend, Ches Smith, Jr. of Atlanta, wrote: "He was without doubt a Good Samaritan in the truest sense. There is no telling how many people he helped through really hard times. He didn't keep score." He was openhanded with his own good fortune. He had a real warmth of heart, a genuine and passionate interest in people, and an anxious desire to do what he could.

He did not honor all personal requests made to him. When a valued black friend asked for help to buy an automobile that he knew she could not support, his reply was, "Mary Ann, who's going to push that wheelbarrow there?"

And when a group of students from the Baptist Home came to the plant for jackets, he told those with long hair to go to the barber first. Some did not go and got no coat.

He would not provide support for buses to transport people to church, feeling they should make it on their own. He also turned down requests from churches for operational expenses, feeling congregations should fund their normal expenses, though they might need help for building a new church or for some other capital outlay.

His secretary said that he could make his mind up about requests "just like that," with the reasons for many of the decisions remaining inscrutable to her. Sometimes he realized that his own instant inclinations about a request could benefit from another's consideration. He attached this note to a friend regarding a reasonably hefty proposal from a college: "I want you to read this letter. I don't want to get into it, but I want somebody to tell me not to."

He never desired recognition for his gifts. A salesman said: "He wasn't a glory hog. He didn't want a lot of praise for the things he did for people." A sewing-room worker said he was a contented man "who saw himself as a receiver of grace" and never wished to be reminded of what he had given.

In addition to his spontaneous personal contributions, which so exasperated his accountant, he employed a number of vehicles for giving. One was the Druid Hills Baptist Church. He channeled tuition money to seminary students through the church, as well as assistance to congregation members in need, such as recent widows or families having members with severe illness.

He gave his pastor, Louie Newton, a batch of signed counter checks for $500, asking him to fill these out as to name and deliver them when deserving cases came to his attention.

A second vehicle for giving was his own staff and salesmen. Occasionally he had a staff member supplied with the same type of checks he gave Dr. Newton and instructed him to keep an eye out for needs in the local area. He of course had his personal advisers concerning all large donations—not that he consistently listened to them.

His widely scattered salesmen brought deserving charities to his attention. For example, a salesman living in Jackson, Mississippi, and on his church's building committee placed Warren Sewell's name down as a possible donor, over protestations of local residents that no one so far away would give more than $25. The salesman bet he would send more than $100, and when the check came it was for $250.

A salesman living in Bremen, also on a church-building committee—this one involving a $300,000 addition to a church that was not Warren Sewell's denomination—spoke to

Pastor Louie D. Newton (right) standing behind seated Warren Sewell.

Warren Sewell about a donation. "What are you giving?" Warren asked. At the response of $15,000 he said, "Put me down for the same." When the church did not reach its goal, those who had pledged were asked again. The salesman put in $6,000, which Warren Sewell again matched. The church got the addition built quickly, before all pledges were due, and needed to borrow $75,000 to pay the builder. When Warren Sewell found out they would have to pay six percent interest, he loaned the church the money interest-free.

In addition to gifts through his church and his salesmen he channeled gifts through the Warren and Ava Sewell Foundation. A formally constituted nonprofit organization, it afforded a means to bestow gifts of a larger size, insuring that tax benefits were received. He gave stock and land to the foundation to sustain it.

His gifts were not always cash. He frequently gave things that had a good market value and high resale value. When he left Atlanta he gave his Springdale Road home and attendant acreage to the Georgia Baptist Hospital.

For local causes such as the Bremen lodge or a school project he had a fund-raising technique. He would host a big steak dinner. Near its conclusion he would get up and say to his guests that he had killed the fatted calf for them and that it was going to cost somebody something. He would then look around the room and say that Sam Hubbard had just pledged so much, Hoyt Broadwell so much, and he would go around the room, "putting the pledge on them." He gave everyone there a figure, even down to one dollar for some. When he finished, he would ask if they had the required sum, and if not, inevitably he would say, "Put me down for the rest."

Warren Sewell had a great belief in local organizations, especially churches, and in their role of caring for local needs. He wanted people in charge of their own environment; he felt they were happier if they had a little authority. People so occupied would do better, keep their farms up, their houses painted, have a better-quality life. The shining prosperity and air of good, self-sufficient living that permeate the area surrounding the clothing plants testify to the merits of his view.

Warren Sewell supported all the churches in his area, of all denominations, both black and white. One of his family ruefully commented that no black church in east Alabama or west Georgia ever painted the church without calling on Warren Sewell first.

Sewell was a tither and saw no reason for a congregation not to make its own operating expenses. As an example of capital outlay, he built a brick church, Bethany, not far out of Bremen on the site of the old Hoggs School. When he occasionally worshiped and spoke there, he always reminded the congregation that their community contained the finest people in the world.

He was charitable but careful also. When the representatives of a country church came to see him, he asked questions about the finances of the church, about the membership. "He weighed us," as a Woodland resident said, "and only after that did he open up his wallet." In most cases he already knew everything about everyone in the congregation. He did not have to do much checking. Few came to him with half-baked requests. Generally after hearing the visitors out he would say, "I want a part in that church" and would give them a check.

He supported the Shiloh Baptist Church near Graham. He had attended there as a youngster and helped to maintain its cemetery, where his parents were buried. A member said that Warren Sewell understandably left his boyhood church and became a member in Atlanta, but that he never left the fellowship of the Shiloh Church nor did he forget it in his gifts.

His interest in churches was matched by an equal interest in students and in schools. At one time, said his pastor, he was supporting twenty-seven college students through the church. The Warren and Ava Sewell Foundation operated a tuition loan program for college students, one with a splendid record for repayment.

A salesman who served on the board of Young Harris College for twenty-two years said he never asked Warren Sewell for money without receiving it at once.

When the steam boiler at Truett-McConnell School exploded, he gave a speedy check for $10,000 to replace it. Tift College, where his first wife Ava went to school, got money for a dormitory.

He served on the local school board and encouraged others to support the schools. A great believer in neighborhood schools, he foresaw some of the problems that would come. For instance, he knew the local black school was not up to par. With donated funds, he arranged for the construction of a new brick school for the black children on Mt. Zion Avenue in Bremen, patterned after the new white school. When it appeared in 1936 that the Bowdon schools, hard pressed for money, would have to close, he gave $15,000.

He gave significant support to Georgia Baptist Hospital, including half a million dollars toward the nurses' dormitory.

Warren Sewell was a vigorous man, accustomed all his life to hard work, long hours, and close management of his business. Until late in his life, his mind remained keen and quick, his memory unimpaired, his hand steady, his energy amazing. But as he grew older, he was not completely well and did not have the stability and strength he earlier had; his mind was simply not as acute. In a firm essentially run by one man, this presented real handicaps, and the business suffered for three or four years.

"As he grew older," said one close associate, "he'd get mixed up about business. And after a meeting he would call to ask what had happened." His workers, having grown accustomed to his energetic presence, were deeply concerned. One said, "We thought it the end of our world." Happily, new leadership brought in after the end of World War II gave the guidance and motivation the business needed and turned it onto a strong course.

Warren Sewell in his later years,
in front of neighbor Sam Hubbard's home, Bremen, Georgia.

Not long after his second marriage he had a stroke, and his condition slowed his travels and his business activities.

Honors and awards, always plentiful, came increasingly to him as he grew older. There was a special celebration for him on his seventy-fifth birthday, 29 October 1963, at Ava Sewell Hall in Bowdon. It started out to be a limited affair—including about fifty business contemporaries, associates, and close friends. But when the plans were explained to him, he asked that there be no selected crowd. When the list was extended to 150 he again said no, for he wanted to ask all his friends.

No written invitations, he said, just ask my friends—everybody—to come and shake hands. More than a thousand of them came to the reception, to greet the man the local paper termed "truly the Bowdon City Father," standing smiling before a tremendous floral "75."

His son-in-law, Lamar Plunkett, presided. Dr. Newton spoke, quoting the First Psalm and Queen Victoria's prayer for Albert, asking the people to "rejoice on the birthday of a great man." Bob Hollomon played the organ to keep the crowd lively, and Emily Carmichael led them in singing "Happy Birthday."

On his eightieth birthday in 1968 there was again a celebration in Ava Sewell Hall, where his daughter, Frances Plunkett, had decorated the foyer with pumpkins, acuba, and flowers in fall colors. "Nine branched candelabra with autumn-gold burning tapers flanked the sides, along with the Georgia flag and the American flag." Finishing the overall picture was a large "80," intricately constructed with flowers.

His family was in the receiving line. His longtime friends Irvin and Alice Kaufman of California came, as well as hundreds of friends from west Georgia and east Alabama. A letter from the town mayor, Lloyd Holloway, was read, naming him "Father of the City."

The birthday celebration began a few days before, when he and his wife traveled in a private rail car to Milledgeville on the Southern and Central "Cancer Special," which con-

Ina and Warren Sewell on his 80th birthday, October 1968.

sisted of twelve private cars. Here there was the premiere showing of a film *The Drum Beaters*, featuring J. Arch Avary and Warren Sewell, in recognition of their leadership in a statewide cancer drive. Sewell had provided free suits to men taking cancer tests.

In October 1972, nine months before his death, he gave an interview for a radio broadcast and was clear of mind and recollection. With astonishing clarity he vividly and in detail remembered events of his childhood, school days, and work as a dirt drummer. He summoned to mind these early times and events when his character was being formed—and with such immediacy that he might have been relating the present rather than recalling the past. His comments show how he cherished the past while being thoughtful of the future. He

Warren and Ina Sewell with Lawrence Welk, Milledgeville, Georgia, October 1968.

expressed deep concern at the drug problem and its effect on the ambitions and lives of young people.

On 16 February 1973 at the West Georgia College homecoming ceremony he was made an honorary alumnus, an award accepted by his son-in-law, Jack Worley, since Warren Sewell was too ill to attend.

After he got really sick he would make a great effort to show up at the plant, even if only for an hour or two. "He just didn't think the day was complete if he didn't make it here," said one worker.

Finally he went to Georgia Baptist Hospital, where he spent three months. As long as he could he wheeled all over the hospital, seeking conversation with any new patient from the Bowdon-Bremen area.

At the age of eighty-five he died on 17 July 1973. On the morning of 19 July his body was brought to the Bowdon Baptist Church, where crowds passed by from eight a.m. until noon, paying respect. A retail merchant who came from Texas lamented that the crowd was so large he could not get in the church.

The funeral service was later that same day in Patterson Funeral Home's Springhill, on Spring Street in Atlanta, with Dr. Louie D. Newton and Reverend Haywood Day officiating. Two of Warren Sewell's favorite hymns were played at the funeral service, "Amazing Grace" and "My Faith Looks up to Thee." In Dr. Newton's tribute he told of Warren Sewell's upbringing by devout parents and of his belief in the "therapy of hard and honest work."

The list of pallbearers reflected his close friends and associates in the clothing business and the community: Guy Darnell, Pat DeHaven, Ed Morris, R. C. Otwell, James Pollard, Mac Smith, Bob Walker, Parks Warnock, Arch Avary, Hoyt Broadwell, D. W. Brooks, Dr. Olin Cofer, John Bill Cook, Roy Davis, Tony DiPlacido, Dr. Albert Evans, Otis Higgins, Sam Hubbard, Gene Hughes, Ridley Lovvorn, J. S. McEachern, E. O. McFather, Dr. Jas. B. Minor, Dr. J. G. Morris, Ed Peel, Will Roop, Ches Smith, Virgil Strickland.

He was buried in Westview Cemetery in Atlanta. Messages of sympathy poured in from all over the country: "The industry has lost one of its pillars," wrote a merchant. The president of a chain of Southern department stores wrote to his son Warren: "Your father and my father were great friends. I can recall many instances when I was a boy that my father called me into his office to meet 'Mr. Sewell, a great friend and a great businessman.' They really enjoyed doing business together."

His pastor wrote later about Warren Sewell: "Drop the plumb line on the life of Warren Palmer Sewell and you read a thrilling story of integrity, fidelity, and abiding satisfaction. He was a Christian gentleman by every finding."

Dr. Newton commented that he had "walked with Warren Sewell, prayed with him, worked with him, fished with him, sorrowed with him, rejoiced with him. I have never seen him look for a short cut, nor heard him whimper under a heavy load. I have so often thought of Micah's words as I saw Mr. Sewell meet and master the issues of life: 'Do justly, love mercy, and walk humbly with thy Lord.' "

His pastor reviewed the many occasions "on which he would hold my hand for the blessing at the table, and how on journeys near and far he would ask me to read some passage from God's word before we knelt in prayer at bedtime."

Uniformly generous-minded and approachable as he was, Warren Sewell was nevertheless a canny businessman and thought deeply about himself, his possessions, his family, his estate, the future. He had a story that he told frequently and perhaps pointedly. It was about an old man who lost his wife and could not live alone. He had three or four daughters and a couple of sons. He transferred his home to one of the daughters and lived with her. First he stayed in an upstairs room, then in the basement, and was always being moved here and there.

He had a sturdy box constructed, put a ten dollar lock on it, and carried it with him everywhere—church, home, bed. He would never say what was in it. When he died, the family rushed home from the funeral to open the box, where they found a hammer and a note reading: "Next old man who gives his home away, hit him in the head with the hammer."

Warren Sewell's children had voting stock in the company, but he retained control. Once he held a stockholders' meeting with the children and their spouses present. Following that session, he never did it again. When he walked in and took off his hat, the board was in session. He would then look around and nod his head, and a decision would be made. One of his staff said: "He held no stockholders' meetings. He had control and he needed it."

Warren Sewell thought long and hard about what to do about his estate. A family adviser said: "He chased this thing through his mind for an awful long time." He wished to avoid turmoil and do the best he could for all and for the stability of the company. He weighed not only the firm but his family—their ages, interests, track records, capacities, potential. In the end he perhaps had no more certainty about what to do than in the beginning. However, with the assistance of his lawyer and his CPA, who were influential in the outcome, he did decide.

He held off distribution of his estate for ten years after his death, leaving it in trust to be managed during the decade by six executors, three of whom were family members and three nonfamily. There was provision that if the executors could not agree, the matter went to the trust department of the First National Bank of Atlanta for handling. Needless to say, this stipulation was a powerful incentive for the achievement of consensus. In effect, he rendered the business independent of any one person.

With only a moderate amount of bickering and controversy, this arrangement carried the company and the family heirs through ten years of prosperity and company growth. Some family members had a knack for selling, some for manufacturing, some for managing, some for all these things. In brief capable family leadership rose to the surface, provided the needed effective management, and kept the firm consistently profitable. In general all were satisfied, though understandably not in every detail.

A wealthy retired Atlanta banker, a contemporary of Warren Sewell, said he was appalled when he heard of the six-executor arrangement: "Even two is bad enough." But he added that under capable leadership it had worked well and been beneficial to the firm. When the estate was distributed ten years after his death, it caused little shift in the management and direction of the firm.

What Warren Sewell did was to chart a long-term course for the business in the hopes that all involved in the firm, including the younger blood, would through experience and work together find a means to continued and effective operation. He had been through one organizational split and knew all about the fears of whether brothers or cousins can merge individual differences and temperaments into a coherent business.

He was not much on fragmentation. He wanted things to move along when he was not there. He arranged for the

Granddaughters (left) Valee Sewell and (right) Kay Sewell and their parents Mary and Warren Sewell, Jr., about 1980.

Grandson Richard Plunkett and Susan Duncan Plunkett, October 1984.

Warren Sewell Clothing Company and Bremen-Bowdon Investment Company to continue to operate and provide a way
of life and living for many people. He hoped that in the decade to come family members would help the business continue and be a source of assistance to the community and its
people. Sewell believed that he had planted good seeds and that
added strength would come. He left the firm free of debt, with
good capital, and in excellent posture for the future.

Grandson Thomas Plunkett and Connie Berg Plunkett.

He had a fondness for stories about family businesses going from shirtsleeves to shirtsleeves in three generations— the first generation working and making it, the second taking, the third breaking it. He prepared for such possibilities by buying continued control of the firm over time through his estate provisions.

One can safely assume that Warren Sewell, viewing today's sprawling and vigorous manufacturing and sales organization, would chuckle at his often-repeated sayings. For the second generation continued to make it, perfecting and embellishing what he started and pursuing his business aims with vigor, personal involvement, and cooperative family spirit. As an example, while he began Bowdon's success, the next generation quietly made the town. Warren Sewell was carefully given all the credit.

His eyes would sparkle at the third generation—that is, both the Sewell family and the Warren Sewell Clothing Company families—at their lives and works, in the business and elsewhere. Well educated—having bachelor's degrees, professional specialties, a master's degree, a Ph.D.—the grandsons and granddaughters have much of their grandfather's nature in them. And they live and labor with the same enthusiastic spirit and family dedication he had.

Warren Palmer Sewell is reaping what he sowed, this diligent First Psalm man, who remains like the tree planted by rivers of water, his leaf not withered, and whatsoever he did still prospering.

Granddaughter Elizabeth Ann Plunkett.

Granddaughter Carol Worley Swindle and Mark S. Swindle, August 1971.

Grandson Robin Worley and Jane Brantley Worley,
September 1978.

Notes on Interviews

The preface speaks of personal interviews being the sources of a large part of this book. The admittedly imperfect listing below is an effort by the author to identify the persons interviewed by placing them into groups that reflect in reasonably simple terms a relation to Warren Sewell. They appear as banking associates, employees, customers, family, farm neighbors, and so on. For clarity a few names appear in more than one category. Some individuals could well be listed in five or six of the groups. When this approach was discussed with Will Roop, one of Warren Sewell's oldest friends, he smiled and said it sounded all right to him, adding "Just put me in everywhere."

Officials, Employees, and Associates, Active and Retired
Warren Sewell Clothing Company

Cole Bell	Eula Norton
Hoyt Broadwell	Raymond Otwell
Avery Cash	Lamar Plunkett
John Cook	L. Richard Plunkett
Richard Daniel	Tom Plunkett
Guy Darnell, Jr.	James Pollard
Roy Davis	Warren Sewell
Helen Feild	J. Mac Smith
Pearl Fowler	Venice Smith
James Garrett	Harris Steed
C. Eugene Hughes	Robert D. Tisinger
George Longino, Jr.	Lee and Lois Waddell
Roy Lee and Sara McClung	Robert Walker
Lowell McManus	Parks Warnock, Jr.
Ed Morris	Gelon Wasdin
Tom Murphy	John Wasdin
Clyde (Buck) Newell	Jack Worley
	Robin Worley

Customers

A. M. Bynum, clothing merchant, Coffeville, Kansas
Irvin Kaufman and Alice Kaufman, Rothchild-Kaufman,
    Los Angeles, California
M. L. Lamar, Austell, Georgia

Bankers

William Bowdoin, Trust Company Bank, Atlanta
Frank Davis, First National Bank of Atlanta
Zelma Harman, Commercial Bank of Bowdon,
Bowdon, Georgia
Virgil Jones, First National Bank of Atlanta
Hardy McCalman, First National Bank of Haralson County,
Bremen, Georgia
J. S. McEachern, Sr., Commercial and Exchange Bank
of Bremen, Bremen, Georgia
E. O. McFather, Sr., Bank of Canton, Canton, Georgia
Will Roop, Bank of Bowdon, Bowdon, Georgia
John Sibley, Trust Company Bank, Atlanta

Business and Industrial Associates

D. W. Brooks, Gold Kist Company
Ted Holmes, Fruit Supplier, Lutz, Florida
Elmer Hubbard, Hubbard Pants Company, Bremen, Georgia
John Hubbard, Hubbard Pants Company, Bremen, Georgia
George Moses, Monroe, Louisiana
Roy Richards, Southwire Incorporated, Carrollton, Georgia
W. Ches Smith, Jr., automobile dealer, East Point, Georgia
George Walls, Dallas, Texas

Cloth and Mill Representatives

Herb Avery, Burlington Mills
Charlie Bligh, Burlington Mills
Harold Friedberg, Peerless Woolen Mills & F. W. Tipper, New York City

Church, Religious, and Charitable Associates

J. Arch Avary, Georgia Cancer Society
Juanita Hughes, Historical Committee, Baptist Church, Woodstock, Georgia
Charles Hudson, Board, Georgia Baptist Hospital, Atlanta
Louis D. Newton, pastor, Druid Hills Baptist Church, Atlanta
Edwin B. Peel, Georgia Baptist Hospital, Atlanta
W. Ches Smith, Jr., Druid Hills Baptist Church, Atlanta
W. Ches Smith III, pastor, Tifton, Georgia
Parks R. Warnock, Sr., staff, Druid Hills Baptist Church, Atlanta

Bowdon Residents

Elfriede Cook, wife of plant superintendent
Jessie Digby and Perry Digby, furniture store owners
Margaret L. Johnson, widow of banker
Norman Lovvorn, retired farmer

Mrs. J. G. Morris, widow of Bowdon College schoolmate
Cope Ozier, businessman and bank director
Will Roop, grocer and banker

Bremen Residents

Marjorie Hubbard, neighbor, widow of clothing
manufacturer
J. Peel Mangham, businessman
Pearl Nethery, neighbor
Pearl Otwell, neighbor
Edgar Rhodes, businessman
Marian Wasdin, widow of Warren Sewell Clothing
Company associate

Carrollton Residents

Edith Foster, librarian
Mrs. J. R. Hamrick, Bowdon College schoolmate
Stanley Parkman, newspaper publisher

Graham Residents

Floy Lovvorn and Pearl Lovvorn, farm neighbors
Curtis Saxon and Ruth Saxon, farm neighbors
Jimmie Stephens, sharecropper on Graham family farm

Atlanta Residents

F. M. Bird, attorney, Alston and Bird
Lois Zumwalt

Wife

Ina Tuggle Morgan Sewell

Brother

Roy B. Sewell

Children and Children-in-Law

Charlotte Sewell Worley and Jack Worley
Frances Sewell Plunkett and Lamar Plunkett
Warren Sewell and Mary Thomas Sewell

Grandchildren

Elizabeth Plunkett
L. Richard Plunkett
Thomas Plunkett
Kay Sewell
Valee Sewell
Carol Worley Swindle
Robin Worley

Nephew, Niece, Cousin, and Other Relations

Lou Darnell, Bremen, Georgia
Helen Freeman, Hendersonville, Tennessee
Inez M. Johnson, Atlanta, Georgia
Ruth Saxon, Graham, Alabama
Grace Sewell, Atlanta, Georgia
Ray Sewell, Sr., Bremen, Georgia
Victor Hugo Sewell, Atlanta, Georgia
William C. Sewell, Newnan, Georgia

THE SEWELL FAMILY TREE

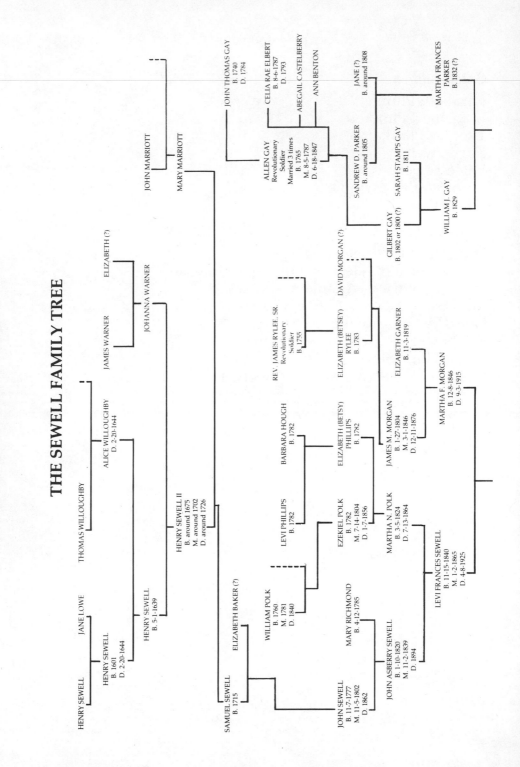

HENRY SEWELL

JANE LOWE

THOMAS WILLOUGHBY

HENRY SEWELL
B. 1601
D. 2-20-1644

ALICE WILLOUGHBY
D. 2-20-1644

JAMES WARNER

ELIZABETH (?)

HENRY SEWELL
B. 5-1-1639

JOHANNA WARNER

JOHN MARRIOTT

HENRY SEWELL II
B. around 1675
M. around 1702
D. around 1726

MARY MARRIOTT

JOHN THOMAS GAY
B. 1740
D. 1784

CELIA RAE ELBERT
B. 8-6-1787
D. 1793

ABEGAIL CASTELBERRY

ANN BENTON

ALLEN GAY
Revolutionary
Soldier
Married 3 times
B. 1765
M. 8-5-1787
D. 6-18-1847

SANDREW D. PARKER
B. around 1805

JANE (?)
B. around 1808

SARAH STAMPS GAY
B. 1811

MARTHA FRANCES
PARKER
B. 1832 (?)

GILBERT GAY
B. 1802 or 1800 (?)

WILLIAM J. GAY
B. 1829

SAMUEL SEWELL
B. 1715

ELIZABETH BAKER (?)

WILLIAM POLK
B. 1760
M. 1781
D. 1840

REV. JAMES RYLEE. SR.
Revolutionary
Soldier
B. 1755

DAVID MORGAN (?)

ELIZABETH (BETSEY)
RYLEE
B. 1783

ELIZABETH GARNER
B. 11-3-1819

BARBARA HOUGH
B. 1782

ELIZABETH (BETSY)
PHILLIPS
B. 1782

JAMES M. MORGAN
B. 1-27-1804
M. 3-1-1846
D. 12-11-1876

MARTHA F. MORGAN
B. 12-8-1846
D. 9-3-1915

LEVI PHILLIPS
B. 1782

EZEKIEL POLK
B. 1782
M. 7-14-1804
D. 1-7-1856

MARTHA N. POLK
B. 3-5-1824
D. 7-13-1864

JOHN SEWELL
B. 11-7-1777
M. 11-5-1802
D. 1862

MARY RICHMOND
B. 4-12-1785

JOHN ASBERRY SEWELL
B. 1-10-1820
M. 11-2-1839
D. 1894

LEVI FRANCES SEWELL
B. 11-15-1840
D. 4-8-1925

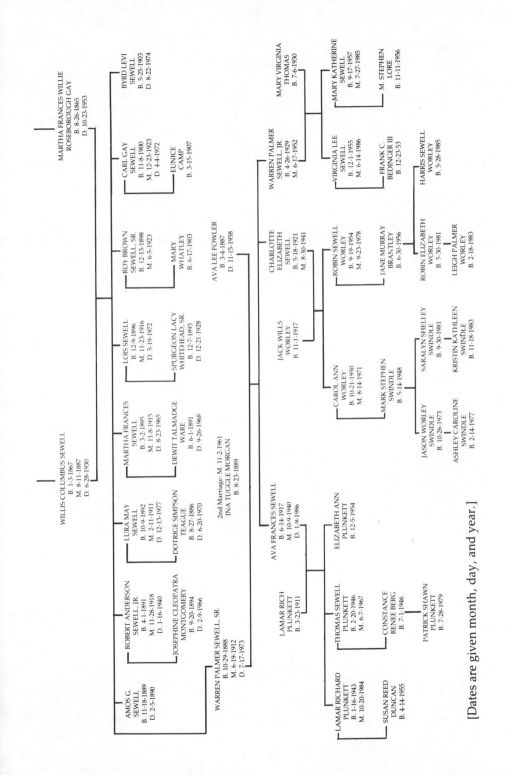

WILLIS COLUMBUS SEWELL
B. 1-3-1867
M. 8-11-1887
D. 6-28-1930

MARTHA FRANCES WILLIE
ROSEBOROUGH GAY
B. 8-26-1865
D. 10-23-1953

AMOS G.
SEWELL
B. 11-18-1889
D. 2-5-1890

ROBERT ANDERSON
SEWELL, JR.
B. 4-1-1891
M. 11-28-1918
D. 1-16-1940

JOSEPHINE CLEOPATRA
MONTGOMERY
B. 9-20-1894
D. 2-9-1966

LURA MAY
SEWELL
B. 10-9-1892
M. 2-11-1911
D. 12-13-1977

DOTRIGE SIMPSON
TEAGUE
B. 8-27-1886
D. 6-20-1968

MARTHA FRANCES
SEWELL
B. 3-2-1895
M. 11-8-1915
D. 8-23-1965

DEWIT TALMADGE
WARE
B. 6-1-1891
D. 9-26-1968

LOIS SEWELL
B. 12-9-1896
M. 11-23-1916
D. 5-19-1972

SPURGEON LACY
WHITEHEAD, SR.
B. 12-7-1893
D. 12-21-1928

ROY BROWN
SEWELL, SR.
B. 12-13-1898
M. 6-5-1923

MARY
WHATLEY
B. 6-17-1903

CARL GAY
SEWELL
B. 11-8-1900
M. 12-23-1923
D. 4-4-1972

EUNICE
CAMP
B. 3-15-1907

BYRD LEVI
SEWELL
B. 5-25-1903
D. 8-22-1974

WARREN PALMER SEWELL, SR.
B. 10-29-1888
M. 6-19-1912
D. 7-17-1973

AVA LEE FOWLER
B. 3-4-1887
D. 11-15-1958

2nd Marriage: M. 11-2-1961
INA TUGGLE MORGAN
B. 8-23-1889

AVA FRANCES SEWELL
B. 6-14-1917
M. 10-9-1940
D. 1-9-1986

LAMAR RICH
PLUNKETT
B. 3-23-1911

LAMAR RICHARD
PLUNKETT
B. 1-16-1943
M. 10-20-1984

SUSAN REED
DUNCAN
B. 4-14-1955

THOMAS SEWELL
PLUNKETT
B. 2-20-1946
M. 6-7-1967

CONSTANCE
RENEE BERG
B. 7-1-1946

ELIZABETH ANN
PLUNKETT
B. 12-5-1954

PATRICK SHAWN
PLUNKETT
B. 7-28-1979

CHARLOTTE
ELIZABETH
SEWELL
B. 5-18-1921
M. 8-30-1941

JACK WILLS
WORLEY
B. 11-1-1917

CAROL ANN
WORLEY
B. 10-21-1950
M. 8-14-1971

MARK STEPHEN
SWINDLE
B. 5-14-1948

JASON WORLEY
SWINDLE
B. 10-26-1973

ASHLEY CAROLINE
SWINDLE
B. 2-14-1977

SARALYN SHELLEY
SWINDLE
B. 9-30-1981

KRISTIN KATHLEEN
SWINDLE
B. 11-18-1983

ROBIN SEWELL
WORLEY
B. 9-19-1954
M. 9-23-1978

JANE MURRAY
BRANTLEY
B. 6-30-1956

ROBIN ELIZABETH
WORLEY
B. 5-30-1981

LEIGH PALMER
WORLEY
B. 2-18-1983

WARREN PALMER
SEWELL, JR.
B. 4-26-1929
M. 6-17-1952

MARY VIRGINIA
THOMAS
B. 7-6-1930

VIRGINIA LEE
SEWELL
B. 12-1-1955
M. 6-14-1986

FRANK C.
BEDINGER III
B. 12-23-53

HARRIS SEWELL
WORLEY
B. 5-28-1985

MARY KATHERINE
SEWELL
B. 9-17-1957
M. 7-27-1985

M. STEPHEN
LORE
B. 11-11-1956

[Dates are given month, day, and year.]

Index

DATE DUE

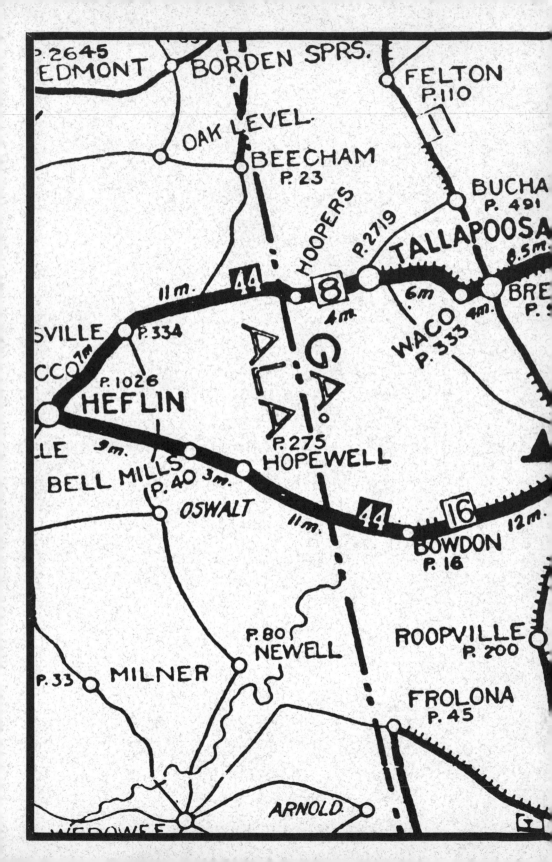